WORLD ON FIRE

How Witches and Wiccans
Transcend the Chaos and Find Their Peace

Moonwater SilverClaw

QuickBreakthrough Publishing

Dedicated to the God and the Goddess and my friends,
family, husband, and you, the reader.

CONTENTS

Title Page

Copyright

Part 1. Facing the Darkness; Finding the Light   2

How Witches Bear the Unbearable   4

How Witches Break Free of Fear   9

How Witches Rise from Being "Broken"   12

How You Can Deal with Anger in Yourself (a Witch's Perspective)   15

How Witches Avoid the Traps of "Common Thought"   18

How Witches Rise Up from the Depths of Despair   23

How Witches Deal with Living in a Scary Future   27

How Witches Deal with Self-Hate Versus Self-Love   30

How Witches Deal with Life When there is No Solution   33

How Witches Deal with Someone Who Won't Hear Them   36

How Witches Handle the Thief of Happiness   38

How Witches Turn Anger into Determination   42

How Witches Deal with the Dark Moments   46

The Witch's Fastest Way to Hope   49

Part 2. The Goddess Embraces You   52

How Witches Walk the Goddess Path While Angry   57

The Raise Your Self-Esteem Meditation   61

How Witches Listen to the Goddess and Take the Right Risk   66

Part 3. Release Yourself from Burdens   69

How Witches Handle When Things are Unfair   70

How Witches Remove Barriers to Happiness   73

How Witches Get to Sleep Even If They Are Angry   76

How Witches Consistently Do Ritual—Beware of the Myth of Motivation   80

How Witches Discover Their Strength in a Crisis   84

Open the Door to the Goddess's Embrace (a Witch's Perspective)   87

How Witches Develop Their Extreme Resilience   89

Heal from Being Broken – a Meditation   95

The InstaCircle   101

The Insta-Ritual   102

Breath of Love   103

The Big Mistake About Going for Wealth and More (a Witch's Perspective)   104

How Witches Keep Their Witch's Vision   108

How Witches Put in Safeguards and Attempt A Spell   111

How Witches Remove the Barriers to Using Magick   114

How Witches Avoid the False Soulmate   117

How Witches Avoid Mistakes They Can't Bounce Back From   120

Part 5. Shift to the Goddess Path   123

Break Through Low Self-Esteem to What You Really Want (a Witch's Perspective)   124

How Witches Stop Fear from Trashing Their Day   128

How Witches Discover What is Spiritually Nourishing to Them   131

How You Can Say "NO" From a Strong Base (a Witch's Perspective)   135

See What the Goddess Reveals (A Witch's Perspective)   138

Embrace Compassion with the Goddess's Viewpoint   140

How Witches Follow the Highest Advice from the Goddess   142

Conclusion: 3 Steps on Your Path with the God and the Goddess   145

Acknowledgement   150

About The Author   152

World On Fire:
How Witches and Wiccans
Transcend the Chaos and Find Their Peace
by
Moonwater SilverClaw

Do you feel things are so much worse now in the world—than ever before?
Wars. Corrupt leadership. Vulnerable people losing lifesaving healthcare. AI destroying jobs.

Imagine you could feel better and even stronger. It's possible. When you apply insights and guidance from the Goddess.

Now is the time to consciously choose how you live each day. Why? Too many people are making profits from getting other people to feel terrible and scared. Social media and broadcast media serve like leeches draining our precious energy.

No more of that. You can separate yourself from the terror of these things.
Call out to the Goddess and the God.

This book is designed to support you during these times of chaos. As you experience this book, you'll discover practical ways to deepen your spiritual experience as a witch. You can find your peace.

Let's begin...

PART 1. FACING THE DARKNESS; FINDING THE LIGHT

Do you feel overwhelmed? Ever have a thought that social media and broadcast media aim to have people feel bad and engulfed in darkness?

You can find the light.
Let's pause for a moment.
Here's a prayer you can use:

Goddess,
Support me to find the light in this moment.
No matter what occurs on the mundane plane,
I know You placed divinity within me.
You delight in my growing and experiencing joy.
So Mote It Be.

In this section of this book, we will explore topics including:

- **How Witches Break Free of Fear**

- **How Witches Rise from Being "Broken"**

- **How Witches Rise Up from the Depths of Despair**

- **How Witches Deal with Self-Hate Versus Self-Love**

- **How Witches Deal with Living in a Scary Future**

With all the unrest in the world, it may feel unbearable. Let's look at a way to counter that.

* * * * * *

HOW WITCHES BEAR
THE UNBEARABLE

Recently, I experienced something new, a stabbing pain in my left knee. It went on for days. So, I went to see my doctor. As part of the healing process, she recommended physical therapy.

Okay. I have begun talking about physical pain. As I write this, I'm enduring back pain.

But many of us are scared for our lives. In this moment, as I write these words, people face their healthcare premiums being doubled here in the United States. Some reports suggest that approximately 11 million adults and children will lose their healthcare all together—in the United States.

The employment of AI continues to destroy existing jobs. Where will all the people go?

It can feel like a reflex to ruminate most of the day or all of the day on these horrible problems.

But what comes of that? Loss of energy, loss of hope. Fear can blind us to anything we can do … or even be grateful for.

So what do we need? Energy. Energy to do what we can.
For example, I just voted. My husband and I studied the material. We had an in-depth conversation, and we gathered the energy to do this. We are also dealing with paperwork for tax preparation. It all takes energy.

For inspiration, let's go to the writing of Doreen Valiente.

She wrote:
In the earth and air and sea,
By the light of moon or sun,
As I pray, so mote it be.
Chant the spell, and be it done!

Doreen invites us to do what we do: Chant, pray, mediate, Cast Circle, conduct rituals.

We can be grateful for Doreen's work. And we can be inspired.

Much of this book is to provide you comfort, inspiration, and support as you call on the God and the Goddess.

You have likely noticed times in life when we must bear the unbearable. It can be physical pain, emotional pain, or both.

Here are three insights.

Insight #1: Protect Your Energy

When my knee acts up, I need to sit down. Standing and walking drain my energy because of the pain.

Another kind of energy drain is emotional — like dealing with a difficult or vicious relative. My friend, Cindy, has a relative who constantly drains her energy. To protect herself, Cindy only interacts with this person once a month.

Some people call this kind of person an energy vampire. But there are others, too:
- **Dream Smashers** — people who shut down your goals and ambitions.
- **Happiness Stealers** — people who suck the joy right out of you.

Some therapists say: You know someone is a true friend if they can genuinely celebrate your success.

But narcissists and energy vampires? They'll find a way to cut you down, especially when something goes right in your life.

Remember: Stay away from those who drain you. Protect your energy.

Insight #2: Welcome New Energy

One way to bring in new energy is through meditation or ritual. You may light a candle and say:
"Lord and Lady, thank you for renewing me with energy."
or
"Thank you, Lord and Lady, for the energy you give me now. Energy that sustains me."

Some people try to conserve energy. They think conserving is enough. We notice the truth: We need to **renew** our personal energy.

On a physical level, something as simple as taking a walk can help bring energy back into your system.

So, do what you can to welcome new energy into your being. Remember: rituals, meditation, prayer, good nutrition, exercise and **sleep!**

You can also gain more energy through my other 9 books – available as ebooks, audiobooks, and paperback books at a major online retailer.

Many people have told me they have gained energy from my 3 courses at Udemy dot com.

Also, you can get the related course to this book titled "World On Fire: How Witches and Wiccans Transcend the Chaos and Find Their Peace" at Goddess Has Your Back dot com forward slash Courses

Insight #3: Let Go Of Negative Expectations

When I first experienced the terrible pain in my knee, I thought, "Is this my new life? Am I always going to feel this much pain?"

In that moment, I was setting myself up with negative expectations.

The truth is: Expectations can either help you or hurt you.

Sometimes I think about a tree growing toward the sun. That tree has a positive expectation. It reaches for sunlight, pulls nutrients from the earth, and continues to grow.

We can have a similar vision for our lives.

On the flip side, we can also fall into a negative self-fulfilling prophecy.

But we have a choice.

I'm choosing to make space for new, positive possibilities.
I've just started physical therapy, and good things can happen.
This is a purposeful action.
I'm letting go of those old negative expectations.

Now I ask you:
Are there things in your life that feel unbearable?

Can you create space to do new things? Will you choose what helps you build up your energy and your peace?

A Prayer to the Goddess
My gracious Goddess,
Help me to protect my energy.
Guide me to gather new energy.
May my expectations shift to the positive and the hopeful.
So Mote It Be.

Let's Pull This All Together

To bear the unbearable, you need good energy.

First, protect your energy.
Second, welcome new energy.
Third, shift your mindset and let go of negative expectations.
Open yourself to positive ones.

* * * * * *

Since we have talked about gaining positive energy, our next move is exploring how to break the chains of fear.

HOW WITCHES BREAK FREE OF FEAR

Alice, a coach I know, teaches managers how to be better leaders. Recently, she had a terrible experience coaching a CEO. Afterward, she told me, "Maybe I don't want to coach other CEOs."

What Alice didn't realize was that fear was in her way.

Here are three insights.

Insight #1: Identify The Trauma

It took a little while—and some conversation—for Alice to recognize what the trauma was. Working with that particular CEO felt like a waste of her time. For Alice, the thought of time brought up something deeper: Her pain from losing three loved ones in the past.

Their deaths made her realize how short life really is. Alice carries fear of wasting her time. That's her trauma.

What happened next is something many of us do: She generalized that trauma. She took the experience with one CEO and applied it to all CEOs. But the truth is, not every CEO is like the one she worked with.

It's completely understandable. We're wired for survival. Human beings naturally try to protect themselves. And, generalizing from trauma is one way we do that.

Insight #2: Recognize When You're Focusing On The Wrong Detail

In her fear, Alice wanted to protect herself. So, she told herself, "I won't coach any CEOs." But that's the wrong detail to focus on.

What she really needed was a way to filter out the kinds of people who might waste her time.

Later, in a conversation with another coach, she had a realization: She doesn't want to work with people who lack compassion or empathy. That's the correct detail.

Fear often makes us focus too narrowly. We go into protection mode. The way to break free of that fear is to have a support system. Use a system with people who can help you identify the right details to pay attention to.

Insight #3: Ask The Goddess To Shift Your Focus

Here's a prayer you can use:

Goddess,
Help me release myself from fear.
Help me identify the trauma that has narrowed my focus.
Guide me to an empowering focus.
Support me to perceive the truth.
And support me to remove the distractions.
Thank You for Your strength, so I may live my best life.
So Mote It Be.

You can use a prayer like this—or something similar—to help you shift out of fear and back into clarity.

Let's Pull This All Together

Many of us go through experiences that create trauma. To protect ourselves, we generalize that trauma. But when we pray or meditate and ask the Goddess to help us shift our focus, something powerful happens. Our perception expands, and we're able to see what really matters.

Remember:
   • Identify the trauma.
   • Recognize when you're focusing on the wrong detail.
   • Ask the Goddess to shift your focus.

* * * * * *

Now that we have seen what happens when we focus on the wrong detail … let's look at anger.

HOW WITCHES RISE FROM BEING "BROKEN"

Do you feel broken?

Many times, I have felt broken. Why? I have depression symptoms. It took me 16 years before I would even call them "depression symptoms." Before that, I would just call myself a depressed person. I had that as an identity. And many of us have identities of being broken.

Here are three insights.

Insight #1: Call Out The Idea Of Being Broken

When something is wrong, many of us will call it out. The idea of being broken, though, is just that—an idea. It's also a label. Did someone in your life label you as something? Just because they gave you a label doesn't mean it's true. It's only an idea. And it's just their idea.

Insight #2: Transform Broken Into A Path

If being broken is an idea, we can transform how we look at that idea. I deal with depression symptoms. Another person might deal with paralysis, or someone else with diabetes. These are things we didn't ask for, but we can choose to find ways to make them our own path.

You might say that our path is a journey to enlightenment. When I first thought about this, I wondered if my depression symptoms journey could be seen as an "assignment." But then I realized a path has more flexibility.

When we look at something as an assignment, it feels imposed on us. We're likely to rebel against it. But a path holds possibility.

Insight #3: Pray To The Goddess For Transformation

Here's a prayer you can use:

Gracious Lady,
Help me transform "broken" into just steps on a path.
Uplift my thoughts so I can see I am worthy.
So Mote It Be.

Let's Pull This All Together

The idea of being broken is just an idea. You can transform an idea, and you can transform being broken into a path. You can also invite the Goddess to support you.

Here is a Quick Recap

- Call out the idea of broken.
- Transform broken into a path.
- Pray to the Goddess for transformation.

* * * * * *

The path we walk is crucial to our lives. It is important to walk a path of strength. Be sure to have skills for handling anger that you feel.

HOW YOU CAN DEAL WITH ANGER IN YOURSELF (A WITCH'S PERSPECTIVE)

I'm angry.
I'm angry at anyone threatening to break down how people receive nessisary life-saving benefits.
Stop attacking people who are in need.

So, what can I do with this anger?

Here are three insights.

Insight #1: Don't Deny Your Anger

I'm really upset. And denying it would only make it fester and beat me up from the inside.
So instead, I look at it. I ask: What good can I do with this?

Also, make sure that you're okay. Do you have enough sleep and support?
Without them, people can break down and do things they regret.
I'm talking about avoiding a denial that you feel anger. I do **NOT** say that it's okay to do inappropriate reactive actions.

As Doreen Valiente noted in *The Wiccan Rede:* "An it harm none,

do as ye will."
It might be necessary to work with a counselor to make sure you and others are not harmed by your anger.

Insight #2: Protect Yourself

I'm helping support family members so they can weather the economic storm.
We're actively looking for ways to increase income and reduce expenses.

Sometimes, anger can be the spark for positive energy and action.
But watch out! Staying angry for too long can wear you down.
Sometimes, you even need to protect yourself from your own anger.

Insight #3: Decide How Much Of Your Day Will Be About Anger

I'm furious about the nessisary life-saving benifits situation in the USA. I could spend an entire day stewing in that anger.

But I have elderly parents to care for. I have my husband, my friends, and my cat, Magick.

These are blessings in my life.
They need me to hold myself together.

I also live with clinical depression. So, I need medication, talk therapy, good nutrition, movement, and solid sleep.

That's why I ask myself daily: How much of my time today will I give to anger?

Insight #4: Pray To The Goddess

Here's a prayer you can use when anger rises:

Goddess,
Give me strength, peace, and insight.
Guide me to use my anger so it supports my path.
So Mote It Be.

Let's Pull This All Together

Researchers tell us that anger itself isn't the problem. It's how we choose to act on it.

We can use anger as a spark to protect ourselves and others, to push for change, and to grow. But we also need support. That might mean therapy, talking with spiritual elders, wise friends, or any combination that helps.

Don't forget: the Gods are there for you.

May these insights support your path.

* * * * * *

We have seen how we can use personal anger as a first step to improving something in our lives. We also saw that other people can be helpful. But when can going along with "common thought" be harmful?

HOW WITCHES AVOID THE TRAPS OF "COMMON THOUGHT"

When my father was young, people didn't understand dyslexia. So, they put a dunce cap on his head and made him sit in the corner. In effect, they called him stupid. And even worse—he believed it. He still believes it to this day.

When I was a small child in kindergarten, I couldn't keep up. I flunked kindergarten. Eventually, I got a diagnosis: dyslexia.

Perhaps, you've heard that many top, highly creative people have learning disabilities—people like Jim Carrey, Whoopi Goldberg, Anthony Hopkins, and many more.

Many of us grow up around people who cut us down. They hold certain "common thoughts," like:
- "Oh, you're different, so you must be bad."
- "You must be stupid."
- "You're probably worthless."

But here's the truth: we must avoid the traps of common thought.

Here are three insights to help guide you.

Insight #1: Pause — Ask, "Is This Really True?"

I face this difficulty every day. I live with depression symptoms. That means bad, harmful thoughts often show up in my own mind.

I'll make a mistake and immediately think, "I'm so stupid."

But I need to pause.
I need to ask for the Goddess's help.
And I need to ask myself:
"Is this really true?"

I also ask for guidance and intuition from the Goddess, because She can see the truth.

If I make a mistake, maybe it's just part of learning something new.
Perhaps, I'm writing something new.
I could be revising a knitting pattern.

Many things that are worthwhile require us to go through some failures.

So, pause, ask yourself if the negative thought is really true, and ask the Gods for Their support.

Insight #2: "How Do I Know This Is True?"

Many of us constantly measure ourselves against others. Some years ago, I heard someone say, **"Don't measure yourself by someone else's best moment."**

On social media, everyone seems to have the best cars, the best meals, the best vacations... and they even look amazing.

But let's be real.

Have you ever seen a celebrity without makeup? She's just a person.

Everything else is manufactured and often photoshopped. Or enhanced by AI. It's not even real.

And that's the point: common thought—like "you should look like this" or "you should have that" can be a trap. People will say, "That's not normal," and make you feel like something's wrong with you.

But you have the power to pause, check in, and ask:
"How do I know this is true?"

When your emotions are being pushed around, that's the exact moment to pause and ask the Gods for guidance.

Insight #3: Ask The Goddess For A New Perspective

Here's a prayer you can use:

Lovely Goddess,
Release me from the traps of common thought.
Open my eyes to new perspectives.
Let me see the way.
So Mote It Be.

It's so easy to fall into the trap of common thought.

Our parents, guardians, and teachers often socialize us to look outside ourselves—and measure ourselves against what the world says is "normal."

But instead, you can use this prayer—or one of your own—and then pause.

Ask the Gods to raise your awareness to the spiritual level, which is far better than common thought.

Let's Pull This All Together

- Pause and ask: Is this really true?
- Ask yourself: How do I know this is true?
- Ask the Goddess for a new perspective.

****

So we learned about fear and to question our thoughts. But what about dealing with despair?

HOW WITCHES RISE UP FROM THE DEPTHS OF DESPAIR

Several years ago, I didn't even know that I was going through despair.

At the time, I was in serious pain in my first marriage. The arguments were constant. Guilt, emotional pain, and so much confusion.

My first husband made me feel like I was broken.

He even used our food money to buy video games. I was hungry. But he wasn't affected. How? *He* kept eating at fast food restaurants.

I was attending community college, trying to build a future, but what I felt was... despair.

Despair is the complete loss or absence of hope. – Oxford Languages

If you're going through something really difficult right now, here are some insights that helped me climb out.

Insight #1: Build Hope

Author Tom Marcoux says, "Building hope is about action and connection."

Some people are great at taking action, but they don't feel connected.

Others might be surrounded by people, but they feel stuck and can't move forward.

In my first marriage, I felt completely isolated.
Eventually, my action was to get a divorce.
That step allowed me to start rebuilding my life.

Once I was free of that painful relationship, I began to heal.
And when I met the man who would become my second husband, I was in a healthier space emotionally.

Hope requires both movement and connection.
You build hope by doing something—and by reaching out.

Insight #2: Build Your Life Preserver (and Keep It Handy)

Wiccan author Scott Cunningham wrote:
"Books can lift our spirits, heal our wounds, steel our courage, and strengthen our religious resolve."

When he writes "steel our courage," he means to make it strong —like metal.

Think of your life preserver as a collection of supportive elements, personal actions and people that help you float. That is, when you feel so much is pulling you under the waves.

For me, my life preserver includes:
- Friendships
- Exercise
- A therapist
- A supportive doctor
- Medication
- My second husband

And yes—books, especially spiritual ones

You rise from despair by filling your life with what is good.

Insight #3: Guard Your Personal Energy

Author Jim Rohn said:
"You can help a thousand people, but you can't carry three on your back."

Who in your life is draining your energy?
That's someone on your back—pulling you down. Exhausting you.

You must protect your energy.

One way to do that is through ritual. I've written about shielding on my blog.
Just go to goddess has your back dot com
and type "shielding" in the search bar.
You'll find posts to help you strengthen your spiritual boundaries.

Insight #4: Ask the Gods for Support

Scott Cunningham also wrote:
"Magick begins in you. Feel your own energy and realize similar energy exists within the earth, stones, plants, water, wind, fire, colors, and animals."

Sometimes life presses so hard on us that we lose hope. And that's when we fall into despair.

This is why it's important to support your relationship with the Gods.

We all have low moments. But when we have a full support system—including our connection with the Divine—we can bounce back more easily.

When I was deep in despair during my first marriage, I had a moment where I felt the Goddess speak to me.

The Goddess said:

"You deserve to be treated better than this."

As a child of the God and Goddess, my destiny was for better. **And your destiny is for better, too.**

When you feel low, here's a prayer you can use:

Goddess,
Help me rise up.
You know there's better for me.
Please support me to rise.
So Mote It Be.

Let's Pull This All Together

Despair is the complete absence of hope.

But every single day, we can work to build hope through:

- Action
- Connection
- Protecting our energy
- Asking the Gods for support

Here's a Quick Recap:
- Build hope.
- Build your life preserver and keep it handy.
- Guard your personal energy.
- Ask the Gods for support.

****

Having hope for things as they are now is great. But what if your mind is living in the future?

HOW WITCHES DEAL WITH LIVING IN A SCARY FUTURE

Recently, someone I know—let's call him Fred—was working with his life partner on her will. As they talked, he began to imagine what life would be like after her passing.

Suddenly, he sobbed.

Fred cried so hard it was difficult for him to breathe.
In that moment, he wasn't just planning for the future—he was living in a terrible one.

This is something many of us struggle with.
Here are three insights to help guide you through it.

Insight #1: Know the Difference Between Living in the Future and Having a Vision for the Future

Fred was living in the future.
He was anticipating great pain, loss, and loneliness. He couldn't imagine a life beyond it.

But here's an important distinction:
Living in the future is NOT the same as envisioning a better future.

For example, many of us who went to college envisioned how a degree could create a better life.

Or when you plan a vacation, you're envisioning joyful experiences ahead.

Living in the future is often rooted in worry.
Having a vision is based in hope and intention.

You can see a big difference between planning and worrying.

Think about these two sentences:
- "I'm worried I'm going to lose my job."
- "I'm planning to move to another state."

Both involve the future.
But one is filled with dread, and the other with direction.

Insight #2: Living Is Done In The Present Moment

Let's bring our conversation back to something simple.

Life happens now.

If you think back to your most cherished memories—those peaceful, joyful, even exciting moments—it's likely that you were fully present in them.

I remember one time when I went snorkeling in the Bahamas.
My husband and I explored sunken treasures and coral reefs. It was magical.
And the magic happened because I was fully there, in that moment.

When you return to the present, you return to life itself.

Insight #3: Pray To Return To The Present Moment

Here's a gentle prayer plus breathing practice you can use

anytime you're stuck in worry or fear about the future.

Presence Prayer & Breath

One breath...
Two breaths...
Three breaths...

Goddess, I am in this present moment.
I am.
I am.
I am here and now.
So Mote It Be.

Someone I know uses a short version:
"Goddess, thank you."
They whisper it when trying to fall back asleep, returning to the now with gratitude.

Simple prayers like these help you return to the present, where your power and peace reside.

Let's Pull This Together

- Know the difference between living in the future and having a vision for the future.
- Remember: living is done in the present moment.
- Use prayer to bring yourself back to the now.

I hope these insights help you live more fully, more peacefully, and more magically—right here in this moment.

Blessed Be.

* * * * * *

We explored envisioning a better future. For many of us, that can feel impossible because we experience self-hate.

HOW WITCHES DEAL WITH SELF-HATE VERSUS SELF-LOVE

Recently, I made a few mistakes while preparing food for a family member. When I realized what I'd done wrong, it sent me spiraling back. Back when I was chastised by my parents, brother, and teachers. It reminded me how often people try to make you feel bad in the name of making you "better."

And the truth is... it works. Making people feel guilty can manipulate them to do what the manipulator wants.
But it also sets up a long-term pattern of self-hatred.

Have you ever had one of those moments where you did something good and felt proud of yourself — only for someone to say, "Yeah, but you still mess up over *here*"?

They don't let you have your moment. It's like they're kicking you for feeling a little bit of self-love.

Here are three insights on how to deal with this.

Insight #1: Authority Figures Use Guilt — And It Sets Up Bad Patterns

Think back to when you were a kid.

Did someone — a parent, guardian, teacher — use guilt to make you feel bad after a mistake?

Yes, guilt can change behavior. But it also plants seeds of shame. As we grow stronger, though, we can shift the script.

You can say to yourself,
"Okay, I made a mistake. I want to do better. How can I do better? Who can help me? Who can coach me?"

You don't need to beat yourself up to grow. You can encourage yourself instead.

Insight #2: The Universe Is Not Binary

Life doesn't boil down to just self-hate or self-love. It's not that simple.
We live in shades of gray — and so do our emotions.

There's self-love, yes. But also:
- self-upset
- self-disappointment
- self-reflection
- self-encouragement

If you catch yourself slipping back into old memories of being chastised, try saying:
"I lead my life now. I encourage myself to grow. If I don't know something, I will find a way to learn."

You are **not defined** by the voices of the past.

Insight #3: Ask The Goddess For Release

Here's a prayer to help you release those old, harmful patterns:

Goddess,
Release me from the spiral of self-hate.
Help me feel the divinity and love within.

So Mote It Be.

Let's Pull This Together

- Authority figures use guilt — and that can create deep, harmful patterns.
- The universe is **not** binary. There's more to your inner world than just love or hate.
- Ask the Goddess for release. You don't have to carry the weight of the past alone.

May these insights support your healing and your path.

* * * * * *

When the world is burning you may think there is no solution. Let's look at that.

HOW WITCHES DEAL WITH LIFE WHEN THERE IS NO SOLUTION

I have a friend, and she is miserable. I care for her very deeply, but there's nothing I can really do to fix her problem. There's no solution. I can't solve it.

What I can do is show up and listen.

Here are three insights for you.

Insight #1: It's Not That There Is No Choice—It's That You Don't Like Your Choices.

This idea about "not liking your choices" comes from the speaker and author Roger Mellott. The point here is to take a wider view of the situation.

I have a friend who lives with chronic pain. The obvious solution would be for the pain to go away, but that's not happening. So instead, it becomes a process of making the best possible choices to maintain mobility. And that includes doing stretching exercises that hurt a lot.

You may have heard of the idea called "the new normal." You

make the best choices you can with your current reality. You adjust to your new situation.

Which brings us to...

Insight #2: Start With Health And Well-Being.

Ask yourself: Are you making choices that protect your health and well-being?

Because we all need time off. Some of us stay up too late, get lost in YouTube shorts, or play video games all night. Watch out. Notice if your habits cause you harm and drain your energy.

As witches, we observe the cycles of the seasons. We see when a fire devastates a forest.

We understand: After a fire, the ash and remains of ash and debris create fertile ground for new life to emerge.

Sometimes we face choices that feel like there's no solution.

I once heard about a man named Sam who had been paying his nephew's living expenses. At a certain point, he said, "I can't do this anymore." And so the nephew had to get a job—and now he's doing quite well.

Do adults need to go through some form of "necessary suffering"? Some authors and researchers suggest that adults often must endure some suffering to have the chance at certain forms of wisdom.

How does that sound to you?

Some forms of healing only happen through hardship. It's like when someone finally ends a terrible relationship. They have to go through the pain before they can grow into something beautiful. They need space in their life to let that happen.

And now...

Insight #3: Pray To The Goddess.

Here is a prayer you can use:

Goddess,
Reveal my real choices.
Show me the way to a true solution.
So Mote It Be.

Let's Pull This All Together

A true solution is one that begins with health and well-being.

So, when it feels like you have no choices, and there is no solution—**find the small, real choices** that help create a foundation of health and well-being.

Because that's what the God and the Goddess want for you.

* * * * * *

Now that you have addressed your health and wellness, consider this situation. Some people simply will **NOT** listen to you. Let's observe some things you can do.

HOW WITCHES DEAL WITH SOMEONE WHO WON'T HEAR THEM

"My sister just won't stop for a minute to hear me out," Milly, a new acquaintance, said.

"She has all these judgments about me and my faith. She doesn't see me as a person. It's like she's talking to her projection of what she thinks I might be."

I reflected on this.

Here are two insights that may help you.

1. You Push, And They Push Back.

Ever try to explain your faith to someone? And, they just push back. Telling you that you're wrong and that they know—better than you—what your spiritual path is.

Arrogant, right?

You push facts, and they push fiction.
But what does the pushing get?
Nothing good.

2. Invite The Gods To Help You Lower Your "Intensity."

Have you noticed that when someone says unfair and ignorant things against you, it's your internal "intensity" that rises?

Here is a prayer that you can use to help you lower your intensity.

I breathe in and bring in the love of the Gods.
I breathe out and let go of my anxiety.
I breathe in and bring in clarity.
I breathe out and let go of my intensity.
I breathe in calm.
I breathe out and let go of my intensity.
I breathe in peace within my integrity.
I breathe out and let go of my intensity.
May the Gods bless me.
So Mote It Be

May these insights support your path.

* * * * * *

Knowing when to cool off and breathe in calm goes a long way. But when happiness is fleeting you may need new insights and actions....

HOW WITCHES HANDLE THE THIEF OF HAPPINESS

For some time now, my friend Sandra has been struggling with her days off from work. Every chore, every errand—it all feels like a heavy burden. Eventually, she realized something important: She felt bad because she was using the words "day off."

But here's the thing—those days weren't really "off."
They were days away from her job, yes, but not free from responsibility. At home, she still had errands to run, bills to pay, and elderly parents to care for. That's not a vacation. That's not time off.

So, for her, the phrase "day off" created unrealistic expectations. And those expectations stole her happiness.

So these expectations acted like a thief of happiness.

But when she started calling them "days away from work," it changed everything. It helped her align with reality—and be more loving toward herself.

Here are three insights that help us, as witches, reclaim our happiness.

Insight #1: Love Of All Beings Includes You

In *The Charge of the Goddess* by Doreen Valiente, the Goddess says Her law is "love unto all beings."

That includes you.

Sometimes, our expectations are the real problem. Sandra's situation is a perfect example: using the wrong words—words like "day off"—set her up for disappointment and resentment.

We witches know: **Words have power. They're spells in and of themselves.**
When we say things like "I should be relaxing," or "this was supposed to be a break," **we may be missing the signs that we're casting a painful spell on ourselves.**

But when Sandra said, "this is a day away from work," **it made space for compassion.** She still had to run errands and help her parents—but she didn't resent it. She was grounded in reality, and that groundedness became an act of self-love.

We can't always change our responsibilities. But we can change how we talk to ourselves. And that's where real magic happens.

Insight #2: Expectations Can Poison Things

Have you ever had a surprisingly good day because you weren't expecting anything?

Let's say it's your birthday. You wake up thinking, "Today has to be perfect." But later, you're stuck in traffic or waiting in line at the grocery store. Suddenly, you're mad. "This shouldn't happen on my birthday!"

But that frustration isn't from the line. It's from the expectation that your day should be flawless.

It helps to loosen up those expectations. Try saying, "I'll enjoy as much of this day as I can."

We witches know that not every spell or ritual is perfect—and that's okay.
The effort, the energy, the intention still matter. **Life isn't about perfection. It's about presence.**

Let go of the poisoned pressure of expectations. They're just another trickster spirit trying to steal your joy.

Insight #3: The Goddess Gives Peace And Freedom

In *The Charge of the Goddess*, we learn that the Goddess's love is poured out upon the Earth, and She gives peace and freedom.

That's why I turn to the Goddess. Not to perfection.
Not to unrealistic expectations. Not to the idea that everything needs to go "just right."

I talk to the Goddess when I feel heavy with responsibilities or disappointed by how a day turned out.

I bring Her my expectations. I ask her:

Goddess,
Cool down my expectations.
Help me return to the present moment.
Help me connect with you.

Because the Goddess is the true source of happiness—not the illusion of perfect days or completed to-do lists.

Let's Pull This All Together:

- Love of all beings includes you. Be mindful of the spells you cast with your words.
- Expectations can poison things. Let go of perfection; embrace presence.
- The Goddess gives peace and freedom. Turn to Her, not to perfectionism.

May your words, your days, and your spirit be filled with compassion.

May the Goddess guide you back to joy.

* * * * * *

The Goddess is **specific** when She states "For My law is love unto all beings…"
But what happens when you still have that deep anger?

HOW WITCHES
TURN ANGER INTO
DETERMINATION

When I was a little girl, my brother—who was three years older and a lot bigger than me—held me under the water in a swimming pool. I was terrified. I truly thought I was going to drown.

But what made it worse was that my mother always dismissed it. She acted like it was no big deal. Like I should just get over it. That made me angry.

Anger can be real. Anger can be justified.
Something was really wrong. A brother isn't supposed to terrify a little girl.

So, what do we do with our justified anger?

Here are three insights for you.

Insight #1: Get Clarity About What You Want

We're talking about turning anger into determination.
Determination comes from knowing what you really want—and being committed to getting it.

So, you must check in with your heart. Ask yourself:
   • Do I want peace, or do I want revenge?

- Do I want peace, or do I want justice?

For example, if someone cuts you off while you're driving, can you really get justice? Probably not. You won't be able to teach that person anything. Maybe it's better to switch to gratitude that you're both alive.

I ask you: What do you really want?

Anger is often a reaction to pain and fear. We're afraid that the bad thing will happen again. So, if you're feeling angry, maybe you need to protect yourself—by setting boundaries or walking away.

That was the case with my first husband.
It was better for me to get a divorce, move on, and stop living in that angry place.

Insight #2: Release The Toxic People

Are you trying to make yourself small just to keep someone else comfortable?

Maybe someone's stepping on you—a coworker, a friend, or even a family member.
We've all heard the term "frenemy." It's important to recognize when someone no longer belongs in your life.

Toxic people drain your energy.
They hold you back. And we witches know: Our lives are about growth and blossoming.

So, if someone is toxic, you need to release them. Even if they were a friend. Even if they're family.

That doesn't always mean cutting them off completely. But it might mean reducing exposure so you can protect your energy.

Insight #3: To Be Determined, You Need a Target

I have a friend, Cindy. People are always surprised by how much energy she has. They ask her, "How do you have so much energy?"

And she says, "I'm always making progress toward my target."

She's an artist. She's always working on creative projects. She's energized because she's aligned with what she wants.

You can ask the Goddess for clarity on your target.

You can use a prayer like this:

Goddess.
Give me clarity.
Guide me to my destiny.
Reveal my target, and help me enjoy my life.
So Mote It Be.

Let's Pull This All Together

Have you noticed that, at times, anger is the right response? Some people do terrible things. And we need to release toxic people from our lives.

But releasing them takes energy. And that energy comes from having a clear target. That's when you know what you want and why you want it.

That's how you transform anger into determination.

Here's a Quick Recap
- Get clarity about what you want.
- Release the toxic people who make you small.
- To be determined, you need a target.

* * * * * *

We *can* be determined. Still, we know that life can be hard to endure. Especially during dark moments...

HOW WITCHES DEAL WITH THE DARK MOMENTS

Are you watching the news wherever you get it, and feeling just awful? It's stunning. It just seems to get worse and worse. And just as I'm feeling really terrible, I notice that Magick, my cat, comes over for snuggles. That changes my focus.

Here are some insights for you.

Insight #1: Focus

How do you wake up each morning? What do you focus on first?

My friend, Jerry, wakes up every morning thinking, "Thank you, God and Goddess, for all the blessings." This means he takes a moment to recognize the blessings he already has. He consciously chooses to focus on what's good in life.

Another person I know replies to "How you doing?" with a positive response. She replies, "I'm breathing. I'm smiling. I'm good."

When we choose to focus on what is good in life, we don't deny the dark moments. We see the whole tapestry of life.

Insight #2: Choose

During real dark moments, it may feel like our choices have been taken away. Health issues, struggles with family, or even heartbreak over global events can leave us feeling powerless.

The truth is, we don't control external events. But our real choice is in how we respond. We can choose to avoid letting a dark moment ruin our entire day.

Here's a quick phrase you can use to shift out of a dark moment: **"Gods, guide me to the light."**

Insight #3: Guiding Light

There's an old idea that we can persist by moving forward, one step at a time. When you see a light at the end of a tunnel, the hard part is choosing what that light will be.

For example, an older person going through a health crisis may focus on something simple: "I'm going to see my grandkids on Saturday." Research shows that many older people stay alive for certain events. They may hold on until a wedding, a celebration, or a meaningful moment.

The point is, choose your own guiding light. Ask yourself: What's important to me? What can serve as my guiding light?

Here's a prayer you can use:

Lord and Lady,
Give me Your light.
Shine it bright upon me for these moments of darkness.
Give me Your guidance and love.
So Mote It Be.

Let's Pull This All Together

Every witch experiences dark moments, and perhaps you're

going through a tough time right now.

Remember: you have choices. You can choose your focus, and you can start your day with gratitude: "Thank you, Gods, for all the blessings."

* * * * * *

We can get our focus back. Now, it's time for some hope.

THE WITCH'S FASTEST WAY TO HOPE

Do you feel hope? Would you call yourself hopeful?

I have a really mixed-up relationship with hope. Recently, I was talking with a friend, and they asked, "When do you feel hope?" My reflex response was, "When my husband has a new lead." A lead is a new prospect so my husband might close a sale.

My friend asked, "Oh, so your feelings of hope are based on something external?"

I shook my head and reflected on this.

Here are three insights.

Insight #1: Wicca And Witchcraft Are Experiential

Sometimes, people who are new to Wicca and witchcraft give up. Perhaps they don't feel hope that they will progress in the Craft. Maybe they think they can read one book, and they're done.

But the Craft is experiential. You need to do things and try things out. When's the last time you did a ritual? Do you have a daily prayer? Have you changed the words of those prayers?

You find your way by walking the path.

Insight #2: Popular Culture Shuts Down Hope

Everything in advertising and social media today seems to promise fun, fast, and easy. People want you to believe that if something is good for you, it will be easy.

This sets a trap. When we encounter resistance, many of us give up, thinking, "It's not worth it."

I've had spiritual elders say, "You're supposed to do rituals at least once a month." At times I felt bad at the Craft because I couldn't manage that.

Since then, I've learned: start small. Don't expect it to be easy. It's all part of the process.

With social media, we're conditioned to jump quickly from image to image, thought to thought. Researchers point out that humans struggle to focus for more than a few minutes.

So, start small. Make your rituals short in duration. Focus on steady, not fast.

Insight #3: Ask The Goddess For Support

Hope is not just an emotion—it's a cognitive process. It's a way of thinking. Your practice of the Craft shapes the way you think and the way you are.

We need to move out of the trap of fun, fast, and easy, and onto **the path of steady, focused, and valuable.**

Here's a prayer you can use:

Goddess,
Let hope shine on me like moonbeams from Your heavenly body.
Support me as I do my hard work in learning the Craft.

May I feel hope in my persistence.
So Mote It Be.

Let's Pull This All Together

Hope is not just an emotion. It's a way of thinking. Hope can be learned. Unfortunately, many of our parents or guardians never learned the hopeful way of thinking.

Hope requires persistence and effort. Invite the Goddess to support you.

PART 2. THE GODDESS EMBRACES YOU

At nineteen, I was getting hell from my mother. She expected me to do more and more. With my depression symptoms, that wasn't possible for me. Depression means less energy. Hello!

But my mother was upside down herself.
She is the queen of denial so it's likely that she had untreated clinical depression, too.
It just meant that she rode me like a jockey.
I had to escape. Just for a little while.

I went on the back deck. I could see trees and even, in the distance, the water of the San Francisco Bay.

I closed my eyes.
I had only tried meditation three times before.
I focused on my breath.
I felt desperate. Overwhelmed. Because she pressed against me, it was like my mother abandoned me and had been replaced with an opponent.

With my eyes closed, I repeated in my mind, "Help me, Lord and Lady."
I kept saying this, internally, with each breath.
I lost track of time.

Did They arrive thirty minutes later or an hour later?
Then, two glowing bits of energy appeared. One on the left, one on the right.

The energy spheres grew. Until the Lord and Lady were full size.
Sitting with the Goddess on my right and the God on my left.
Then I noticed that They held my hands.
I didn't need to say anything.
With the presence of the God and Goddess, the darkness of my depression symptoms disappeared.
They did not have to say anything.
I just *knew.*
Beyond words, They expressed that I was worthy, beloved, and good.
The divinity in me resonated with the divinity in Them.
They had placed divinity in me, and the details of the mundane plane including my depression symptoms and loneliness lost their impact.
I had never felt so valuable and loved!

I always remember this experience. I am deeply grateful to the Goddess and God for embracing me.

In this section, we will explore topics including....

- How Witches Deal with "Am I Good Enough?"
- How to Walk the Goddess Path While Angry
- The Raise Your Self-Esteem Meditation

Let's continue...

How Witches Deal with "Am I Good Enough?"

How do witches deal with that big question: "Am I good enough?"
Is there a perfect ritual to fix this?
Not really.

Do you struggle with this question "Am I good enough"?

I do.
Every day, I feel like I'm not good enough.
Can you relate?

Here are three insights.

Insight #1: Good Enough Is Not Perfect

Recently, my husband asked me, "When have you felt good enough?"

And my response was, "I'm not perfect."

But that wasn't the question, was it?

We often confuse "good enough" with "perfect."
But the two are *not* the same.

And even then—good enough compared to what?

There's an old saying:
"Don't compare your inside with someone else's outside."

Many people appear perfect or special on the outside... especially in manufactured images for social media.

However, we hear reports that a number of celebrities endure personal fear and self-doubt.

And having fear or doubt doesn't mean you're not good enough.
It simply means you're having a human experience.

Now imagine:
You're beyond this incarnation, in the Summerlands, free from distractions of the body.
There, you can feel your worth and sense the Divinity the Gods placed within you.

But here, on the Earthly plane, we deal with bodies, emotions, doubts... and still,
we can be good enough.

Insight #2: Act As If You're Good Enough

I was recently speaking with some spiritual elders.
I shared how my depression symptoms make me feel terrible a lot of the time.

I realized something important:
I can't wait to feel good enough.
I must act as if I'm good enough.

For example, a company did something wrong. They made a false charge on my credit card. It took months of persistence to get it resolved.
Even though I wasn't feeling strong or confident, I had to stay assertive. I had to act.

That's the key.
You act as if you're good enough even when you don't feel like it.

Depression symptoms often act like a filter.
They block out the positive.
They make it harder to hold onto good memories.

So, to live the life I want,
I must act as if I'm good enough.

That means being an advocate for my elderly parents.
I talk to their doctors, make appointments, and speak for them at their care facility.

From the outside, someone might think I have high self-esteem.
But I'm just acting as if I do because I must.

How would your life improve if you acted as if you are good enough?

Insight #3: Pray To The Gods

Part of acting "as if" is nurturing your relationship with the

Gods.
Even if you don't feel worthy—pray anyway.

Here's a prayer you can use or adapt:

My Worthiness Prayer
Lord and Lady,
Reveal my worthiness.
Wipe away all distractions from my mind.
Sow positive thoughts in mine.
Support me to know the Divinity You placed within me.
So Mote It Be.

Sometimes, when you're not feeling strong, the best thing you can do is pray.

Let's Pull This All Together

- Good enough is not perfect.
- Act as if you're good enough.
- Pray to the Gods.

* * * * * *

We are good enough. We have the Gods in us. But what if we are walking the path in anger?

HOW WITCHES WALK THE GODDESS PATH WHILE ANGRY

The last time I felt truly angry was with a family member who was irritable in the morning. Their energy affected me so deeply that I withdrew. I didn't want to be around them.

This experience led me to reflect deeply.

Here are three insights on how to walk the Goddess path during challenging emotional moments.

Insight #1: Identify Venting, Complaining, And Anger

Not long ago, I had a conversation with a spiritual elder, and we explored three related but very different experiences:

- Venting
- Continuous complaining
- Practicing anger

Venting can actually be healthy when it has boundaries. For example, you might set a timer for 10 minutes to talk about what's bothering you. That's intentional. It is what I call "release with structure."

But continuous complaining is different. That's when we keep replaying the same negative moments. It drags us down. It can drag our friends and loved ones down with us.

And then there's something even deeper: *practicing anger.* **That's when anger becomes a habit.** A mode of being. That can turn someone bitter over time.

It's important to reflect on which of these patterns we're engaging in. Once we identify them, we can begin to bring the Goddess into our process.

Insight #2: Connect With Two Specific Aspects Of The Goddess

As witches, we often work with the three aspects of the Goddess:
  - The Maiden
  - The Mother
  - The Crone

In the context of anger, two aspects can be especially powerful:

The Mother
The Mother is the nurturer, the creator. When you're angry, you often need nurturing and the creative power to find solutions.

The Crone
The Crone is the wise one. She helps you harvest wisdom from your life experiences, even the painful ones.

Often, our anger is rooted in fear.
  - Fear of being treated badly and not being able to stop it.
  - Fear of losing your place, your power, or your peace.
  - Fear that if you don't speak up, things will only get worse.

Anger itself is not evil or wrong. But what we do with our anger is where the Goddess can guide us.

Insight #3: Use A Chant To Connect With The Goddess

So far, we've talked about venting, complaining, and practicing anger. We've looked at the nurturing and wise aspects of the Goddess. Now let's bring it all together with a chant. It's a spiritual tool to shift your energy and call on Divine support.

You can use this chant when you feel yourself overwhelmed by anger:

Goddess
Help me nurture like the Mother,
And gain wisdom like the Crone.

This chant is more than just words. It's an energetic shift. You're choosing to change your thinking. You're asking the Goddess to help. And She will. She *wants* to help you.

When you experience anger, **it's not just emotional. It's a call to your soul.**
Something needs healing. Something may need to change within you, or in the world around you. Calling on the Goddess is a sacred step toward transformation.

Let's Pull This All Together

- Identify venting, complaining, and practicing anger. They're not the same. They need different responses.
- Connect with two aspects of the Goddess: The nurturing Mother and the wise Crone.
- Use a chant to center yourself and call in Divine support.

May your path be guided, even in anger. And may the Goddess walk with you through all your emotions. She can guide you through the fire to true healing.

* * * * * *

We can stay on our true path, even when experiencing a form of anger.
Some authors and spiritual elders mention that supporting one's self-esteem is valuable.
I appreciate this definition of self-esteem:

"Self-esteem is the experience of being competent to cope with the basic challenges of life and of being worthy of happiness." – Nathaniel Branden

I developed a "Raise Your Self-Esteem Meditation."
May you find value in it…

THE RAISE YOUR SELF-ESTEEM MEDITATION

Welcome to this meditation.

You can record yourself as you read this meditation into a recording device. Perhaps, you might use a smartphone.

Then, when you designate a time to do the meditation, pause. Make sure you are in a safe place where you will not be disturbed. Turn off your phone's ringer and any alerts.

Now, let's begin.

Begin to Relax.
Close your eyes.
Take a deep breath in.
And exhale slowly.

Breathe in deeply again.
And release all the stress of the day.
Inhale peace.
Exhale tension.

You are still aware of the light in the room.
As that light begins to gently fade, you feel yourself surrounded by comfort.
You are safe and secure in this peaceful darkness.

Now, a new light begins to form.

You feel warmth and deep safety in this light.

Soon, you notice a stairway before you.
You gently take hold of the banister.
Take a deep breath... and step down.

Your worries begin to drift away.

Breathe in... and out...
Take another step down.
Your mind becomes quiet.

Breathe in... and out...
Step down again.

Your shoulders, face, and head begin to relax...
Your arms soften.

Breathe in deeply... and exhale.
Step down again.

Your chest, stomach, and legs all begin to relax.
Breathe in... and out...
Step down again.

Your mind is now at ease.

Breathe in...
Breathe out...
Step down again.

Your body is now completely relaxed.
You step down one final time. Your feet are now on the sand of a beach.

You now find yourself at the bottom of the staircase, looking out at the ocean.

Waves gently lap against the shore.
The sun is setting.
It is beautiful.

You feel peace and comfort here.

And then… you feel a deep inner knowing.

You realize:
Your worth is based on the Divinity placed within you by the God and Goddess.

You now realize that your self-esteem is about recognizing your capacity to handle the tough parts of life. You can learn what you need to.
You have Divinity placed within you by the God and Goddess. So, you have talent and capacities to learn. You have capacities to get stronger and make healthy, empowering decisions.

The God and Goddess support you in this incarnation.
They celebrate all that you learn.

Your divine path is learning.
You have faith in the God and Goddess—
and because They placed divinity within you,
you now have faith in yourself.

You understand that it is natural in this incarnation to make mistakes.

Each mistake is like a streetlamp—
revealing something new to learn.

Learning is natural for you.

This incarnation is your classroom,
and the Gods smile upon your efforts.

You now feel your abilities more clearly.
You feel confident in your gifts.
You know your worth is divine.

Your worth comes from within.
If someone outside says something negative—

it cannot touch your inner divinity.

You are a part of the God and Goddess.
And because of this:

You are worthy.
You are strong.
You are eternal.

You take three deep breaths.

Inhale... taking in the love of the Gods.
Exhale... releasing all doubt.

Inhale again... filling with Divine love.
Exhale... letting go of any remaining fear.

And one more deep breath...
Breathing in Their light and love.
Breathing out any lingering doubt.

You feel serene, and one with the Gods.
You know you are valuable.
And the Gods know it too.

Now, you sense that it's time to return.

The light begins to fade... slowly at first.
It becomes darker... and darker...
You are still safe in this peaceful darkness.

Then, another light appears.
It grows brighter...
and brighter...

And you realize:
This is the light of the room where you began.

You know you will carry this good feeling with you.
You can come back here anytime you wish.

And you will carry the love of the Gods within you

as you go through your daily life.

When you're ready...
Gently open your eyes.

This completes the meditation.

* * * * * *

With the Raise Your Self-Esteem Meditation, you have had an experience of your true worth—the Divinity placed by the God and Goddess within you.
The Goddess supports you. She can guide you to take the right risk.

HOW WITCHES LISTEN TO THE GODDESS AND TAKE THE RIGHT RISK

I have a friend, Jeremy, who's feeling confused. Should he stay in his current job? It's hard work, but it's steady. Or should he go after a new opportunity that he's unsure about—one that actually scares him?

It would be a big risk. And like many of us, Jeremy's not sure what the right move is.

Here are three insights.

Insight #1: Only Through Risk Will You Learn The Unknown

In the writing of Doreen Valiente, the Goddess, says:

"To these I will teach things that are yet unknown."

These words come from *The Charge of the Goddess*. They speak to magickal knowledge. The words also apply to our everyday lives, especially when we're standing at a crossroads.

Only by taking appropriate risks can we open ourselves to new experiences, new wisdom, and new possibilities.

Think of a baby who might think, "Crawling is fine. Why risk walking and falling?" But with the guidance of the Goddess, life is about stepping into the next level of growth. And every level comes with its own kind of risk.

Remember: *"To these I will teach things that are yet unknown."*

For Jeremy, the next step is ritual and meditation, to listen for the Goddess's guidance. This will help him discern whether the new job is the right kind of risk. Not every risk is the right one. It helps to gain the Goddess's guidance. Then, you can flow beyond fear.

Insight #2: Get Free from the Slavery of the Ego

The ego is that part of us that feels small and afraid. For Jeremy, it might whisper, "What if you fail? What if you look foolish?"

But the truth is, he is not his ego. He is a child of the Goddess.

Even if the new job doesn't work out, he doesn't have to put it on his resume! But he might learn something incredible. Something he couldn't have learned by staying where he is.

The ego wants comfort. It wants to hide, to stay small and safe. But that's not what the Goddess wants for us.

The Goddess wants us to expand. To grow. To be brave.

In *The Charge of the Goddess*, She says:
"Ye shall be free from slavery."

I believe this means freedom from the slavery of the ego. The ego is the part of us that keeps us from fully living.

Insight #3: Keep In Mind The Goddess's Teachings

Here's another passage from *The Charge of the Goddess* that I love:
"Keep pure your highest ideal. Strive ever toward it. Let naught stop

you or turn you aside."

So, in this conversation about risk, we come back to three core teachings from the Goddess:
- To these I shall teach things that are yet unknown.
- Ye shall be free from slavery.
- Keep pure your highest ideal. Strive ever toward it. Let naught stop you or turn you aside.

These are powerful teachings. And if life has felt hard for you, as it has for me at times, you may find comfort in them, too.

When we hold the Goddess's lessons in our hearts, we find strength. We rise. We embrace the risks that are meant for us. And we return to ritual and meditation to hear Her voice.

Her voice is one of encouragement. It sounds very different from the voice of fear that says, stay hidden, stay small.

One More Thought On Risk

When you take a risk, make sure you have a support system in place. And include the Gods in your process.

A daily spiritual practice can help: Ritual, prayer, and meditation. Even a two-minute meditation is enough to begin building the connection and clarity you need.

Let's Pull This All Together

Here are the three insights:
- Only through risk will you learn the unknown.
- Get free from the slavery of the ego.
- Keep in mind the Goddess's teachings.

* * * * * *

PART 3. RELEASE YOURSELF FROM BURDENS

What burdens are upon your shoulders now? Do you feel that life has slammed you with unfair situations?

Do you even carry burdens of exhaustion and self-doubt?

Turn to the Goddess, through ritual, meditation, and prayer. The Goddess can give you relief. She provides the renewal of your personal energy.

In this section, we will explore topics including:
- Handle When Things are Unfair
- Remove Barriers to Happiness
- Get to Sleep Even When You Feel Angry

Let's continue…

HOW WITCHES HANDLE WHEN THINGS ARE UNFAIR

Years ago, during my first marriage, one day my ex-husband became extremely angry and verbally abusive toward me. Fortunately, I had already developed a consistent meditation practice.

So, when he started yelling at me, I raised my shield. By shield I mean an energy barrier between him and myself.

Suddenly, I felt relief. His negative energy wasn't getting through. It wasn't penetrating my shield.

Here are three insights.

Insight #1: Protect Yourself With A Shield

In a world full of unfairness, it's absolutely necessary to practice raising your shield.

Have you noticed that so many people walk around twisted and upside-down inside? You can't let yourself be a punching bag for their pain. But at the same time, you don't want to descend to their level either.

Why? Because their level is misery.

Raising your shield is a process. It includes meditation and intention-setting. You might say something like:

"I'm raising my shield so that only love may enter in. All negative energy is blocked."

Insight #2: Use Grounding

Grounding is another powerful tool. It often includes meditation. You can visualize any negative energy being pulled down through your body and out through your feet. The negative energy is shunted harmlessly into the Earth.

Let Mother Earth absorb it.

When you're dealing with unfairness, you need to keep your energy calm. Grounding helps you do that.

Insight #3: Refresh Yourself With Energy From The Gods

So far, we've talked about using a shield to block negative energy, and grounding to release what's already inside of you. Both are important because unfairness can stir up a lot of upset, anger, and stress.

You ground yourself. That helps you empty negative energy. Now there's space.

That space can be filled with Divine energy.

You can pull in the Gods' energy from the universe, drawing it down through your crown chakra, and filling all the places that were cleared during grounding.

These practices of shielding, grounding, and refreshing yourself with Divine energy work together. They elevate your consciousness.

But it takes practice. It takes consistency.

You have to condition yourself so that when an unfair moment comes, you're ready. Over time, with regular practice, you'll become faster and stronger with these techniques.

It's like having a toolkit always ready. This is one that you carry inside yourself.

Let's Pull This All Together:

- Protect yourself with a shield.
- Use grounding to release negative energy.
- Refresh yourself with energy from the Gods.

* * * * * *

We talked about using a shield to protect you from negative energy. On the other hand, you may find that you have some barriers to letting yourself experience happiness...

HOW WITCHES REMOVE BARRIERS TO HAPPINESS

Recently, I was knitting, and it just didn't feel the same. It wasn't bringing me the joy it used to. I kept making little mistakes, and I realized my focus just wasn't like it was in previous years. That really bothered me.

Knitting used to be a source of happiness. But now, something felt off.

Here are three insights.

Insight #1: Observe Your Focus

As I sat and knitted, I noticed the pattern wasn't coming out quite right. And immediately, I started criticizing myself. That was the easy part. Because I live with symptoms of depression.

So, the first step was **Observe your focus.**

For many of us, negative thoughts show up every single day. I'm not saying we have to get rid of all of them. That's not realistic. But we can start by noticing where our focus goes.

Are we stuck in criticism? Are we focusing on perfection or productivity instead of enjoyment?

Insight #2: Be Selective And Choose

We don't always control that first thought that pops into our head. But the second one? **That's where we have a choice.**

Going back to my knitting. My first thought was "I'm doing this wrong." I could let that spiral downward. **Or I could choose a second thought like, "I'm just doing this because I enjoy it. I'm not performing for anyone."**

Knitting doesn't have to be perfect to bring peace. It's an activity that adds quiet contentment to my life.

My sweetheart is a great example of this. He often assembles physical jigsaw puzzles. He doesn't count them or track them. It's just a meditative thing he enjoys. But when he writes, that's different. He does track the pages. Because that's where his focus is more structured.

So, again: **Be selective. Choose your second thought.**

You observe your focus, then you consciously select your next thought. That's where your power is.

Insight #3: Focus On Giving To The Gods

We receive blessings all the time, but how often do we pause to give something back?

Here's something important to remember: your relationship with the Gods is a flow of give and take. The Gods enjoy our happiness.

The act of giving to the Gods actually nurtures our own contentment. When I light candles for my deities, I'm offering something simple but meaningful. They feel the energy of the candle, and the energy of my intention.

Giving becomes a spiritual exchange. It reminds us that we're in relationship with the Divine, with the world, and with ourselves.

Let's Pull This All Together:

- Observe your focus.
- Be selective—and choose your second thought.
- Focus on giving to the Gods.

* * * * * *

You notice we talk a lot about focus in this book. Your choice of focus is important for a witch. This comes into play when getting to sleep, too. You move your thoughts and shift them to something else.

HOW WITCHES GET TO SLEEP EVEN IF THEY ARE ANGRY

The other day, I was just doing my regular grocery shopping. I had finished up and was putting my bags into my car. I heard honking behind me. At first, I didn't think anything of it. It was a parking lot. But eventually, I turned around and saw a woman in her car, honking directly at me.

I caught her face as she glared at me, and the look on it was... entitled. She was treating me like a servant who needed to move faster.

That really pissed me off.

Now, I'm aware of **the Threefold Law**. As a Wiccan, I don't send out negative energy. But the problem was, this anger kept bubbling up all day long. And by nighttime, it was still with me. It was interfering with my sleep.

Have you ever been so angry that it interfered with your sleep? Or do you suffer when tortured by ruminating thoughts?

Here are three insights.

Insight #1: Shift From Anger To Gratitude

We begin by calling on the Goddess, and we create a simple

mantra. One that works beautifully is:

"Goddess, thank you."

You repeat this mantra over and over in your mind. *Goddess, thank you. Goddess, thank you.*

Now, your first thought might be, Thank Her for what? For the woman who honked at me and made me feel small? But here's what happens: **When you say "thank you," your mind naturally begins looking for things to be grateful for.**

It could be as simple as:
- I'm breathing.
- I can walk.
- I can see and hear.
- I still have people in my life who love me.
- Or even, I'm grateful for the time I had with a loved one before they passed.

Something to be grateful for is present. We just need look gently and patiently.

If you're still struggling, try counting down from 10 to 1, and pair each number with something you're thankful for:

10. I'm breathing. Goddess, thank you.
9. I can see. Goddess, thank you.
8. I'm so grateful for Susan. Goddess, thank you.

Once your mind starts connecting to gratitude, return to the mantra: *Goddess, thank you.*

Repeat it 21 times in your mind, gently and slowly. You may find that your mind gets bored. That's exactly what we want. Boredom lets you drift into sleep.

Insight #2: Shift To Beyond Words

Sometimes words keep our minds too active. So, in this practice, we shift away from verbal thinking and into sacred sounds.

On your inhale, silently think of the sound: *Ah*
On your exhale, silently think of the sound: *Om*

These sacred sounds are found in Divine names like Goddess, God, Buddha, and others. The "ah" sound connects to divinity, and "om" brings peace.

Try it now:
Inhale: *Ah*
Exhale: *Om*

Again:
Inhale: *Ah*
Exhale: *Om*

Do this silently, inside your mind. Feel how the rhythm begins to slow your thoughts and your body.

Insight #3: Move Slightly To Move Your Mind

This technique is borrowed from the Navy SEALs—something they use to fall asleep quickly, even on helicopters heading into combat. It's called progressive relaxation.

They work through their whole body, tensing and releasing each part. Let's try a simple version of it right now.

If you're in a safe and quiet space:
Start with your hands. Make fists and tighten them.
Now, tense your forearms.
And then... *release.*

You're working with your body to quiet your mind.

Here's another version of the same idea:

Lie comfortably in bed. Place your palms downward.

On your inhale, slightly lift your index finger and in your mind say:
Goddess.

On your exhale, relax your finger back down and say:
Thank you.

You can combine this with the sacred sounds from before:

Inhale: *Ah* (finger lifts slightly)
Exhale: *Om* (finger relaxes and settles on the bed)

These small movements anchor your mind in the present moment. They help you gently pull away from spiraling thoughts.

Let's Pull This All Together

Even when you're angry or struggling with racing thoughts, you can still fall asleep. These three insights form your toolkit:
- Shift from anger to gratitude.
- Shift beyond words into sacred sounds.
- Move slightly to move your mind.

You're not trying to force yourself to sleep. You're gently guiding yourself into it. You use the body, breath, and spirit together.

May these practices bring you peace and deep, restful sleep.

* * * * * *

Sleep is essential to a healthy life. On the other hand, sometimes, people get caught up in an unhelpful myth. This can cause discomfort. Let's talk about a myth...

HOW WITCHES CONSISTENTLY DO RITUAL—BEWARE OF THE MYTH OF MOTIVATION

Let's start with something big and important: **Beware of the Myth of Motivation.**

Ask yourself—are you doing ritual every week?

I'll admit, I don't always get ritual in.
When I don't, I don't feel great about it.

I was talking to a spiritual elder about consistency in practice, and about motivation... and that conversation gave me three insights I'll share with you.

Insight #1: You Don't Get Better At The Craft Without Consistent Practice

Performing ritual and casting Circle is like anything else, you need to practice. It needs to become familiar. It needs to become second nature.

Any athlete knows this. A basketball player doesn't dribble the ball by overthinking it. They've done it enough times that it becomes automatic.

Here's a progression when you're learning something new:
- **Unconscious incompetence:** You don't know what you're doing, and you don't even know that you don't know.
- **Conscious incompetence:** You start to realize your mistakes.
- **Conscious competence:** You know how to do it, but it still feels awkward.
- **Unconscious competence:** It becomes part of you. You no longer have to think about it. You just do it.

That's where we want to be with ritual. But to get there, you need consistent practice and the right training.

Insight #2: Replace The Myth Of Motivation

How many times have you thought, "I'd do that... if only I feel motivated."

Waiting to feel motivated? That's a trap. It's unreliable. Sometimes motivation never comes. Or it comes right before bed when it's too late to act on it.

I know someone who's written over 55 books. He doesn't wait to feel like writing. He has two things: Focus and systems.

So, ask yourself: How can you build a system that supports your Craft?

Here's an example from my own life. I wanted to change how I felt in the morning. So, I wrote a morning prayer, printed it out, and placed it on top of my laptop. I won't let myself check the Internet until I read the prayer out loud.

Simple. Effective. That's a system.

So how can you build a system that makes ritual part of your daily or weekly rhythm? Something that removes the need for motivation and replaces it with momentum?

Insight #3: Ask The Gods For Support

Are you going through a hard time right now? Feeling like it's hard just to hold things together?

You don't have to do it alone. The Gods are with you. You can pray. You can ask for help.

You can use your focus and your systems. Also, **lean into your relationship** with the Divine.

Here's a prayer you can use:

Lord and Lady,
Help me create a system that I can use.
To make ritual a natural part of my week.
So Mote It Be.

Let's Pull This All Together

- You do not get better at The Craft without consistent practice.
- Replace the Myth of Motivation with systems and focus.
- Ask the Gods for support, spiritually and practically.

Let these insights guide you in bringing ritual more fully into your life. You don't have to wait for motivation. Ritual can become something natural, powerful, and deeply woven into your week.

* * * * * *

We've talked about placing good practices into your daily life. But what if you are slammed with a surprising crisis?

HOW WITCHES DISCOVER THEIR STRENGTH IN A CRISIS

What can witch's do when a crisis slams into their life?
Do you feel overwhelmed?
Would you like to feel relief and receive help from the Gods?

Here are three insights.

Insight #1: Receive The Strength Of The Gods

At one time, I really needed help. I faced something important and life-changing. It was scary. I was anxious, and I didn't know what was going to happen. So, I turned to prayer. I called on the Gods many times throughout the day.

And something happened.

Through those prayers, I felt a bit of peace. Then I felt hope. And in the end, I did receive the benefits I needed.

Imagine what it would be like to bring that into your daily life. You say prayers to the Gods throughout your day, again and again. Not out of fear, but out of trust.

This kind of connection changes you. It deepens your relationship with the Divine.

Insight #2: Trust That There Is A Reason

Another time in my life, I had to move. I didn't want to. It was sudden and unsettling. I had no idea where I would go. But circumstances pushed me forward.

And as hard as it was... that move turned out to be the beginning of a beautiful new chapter in my life.

Now I can look back and see the hands of the Gods in it all. They were moving me, not to punish me, but to position me for something better.

So, I ask you:
- Can you imagine what new chapter might be in front of you?
- Is it possible the Gods are preparing you for something more?

Insight #3: Use The One With Deity Chant

Sometimes life is so overwhelming, we need something simple. Something we can hold onto in the moment. A chant can be like a flashlight in a dark room.

I wrote a chant called the *One with Deity chant.* It helps connect you with the Gods and with your own inner strength.

One with Deity Chant
I trust in the Gods.
I trust in myself.
We are one and at peace.

Find a safe place.
Say it out loud.
I trust in the Gods.

I trust in myself.
We are one and at peace.

You can start by saying it three times. Maybe build up to six. Or even nine times, whatever feels right to you. Three is a sacred number, and nine is three times three. Let the repetition deepen your focus and your connection.

Use this chant whenever you need it—when you're scared, when you're angry, when you're uncertain. Let it remind you that you're not alone.

And over time, build your own daily routines that help you connect with the Gods.

Let's Pull This All Together

- Receive the strength of the Gods. Let them carry you through.
- Trust that there is a reason. Even in hard times, something sacred is unfolding.
- Use the One with Deity chant to stay connected and grounded in Divine peace.

These tools are here for you. The tools are simple, powerful, and sacred. May they guide you through any crisis and lead you back to your strength.

* * * * * *

Getting through any crisis is a stretch. Now we have a transition. Now we will open ourselves to the Goddess's Embrace.

OPEN THE DOOR TO THE GODDESS'S EMBRACE (A WITCH'S PERSPECTIVE)

My parents dragged me, as a little girl, to Sunday church services. Often, the church leader would talk about how wretched the people in the chairs were. They had to be wrecks so they would need to be "saved."

I could feel my head shaking. Even at eight years old, I knew this was **not** my group. This was **not** where I belonged.

Over the years, I've learned that a primary way to feel the Divinity the Gods placed in you is to go to the place of "letting go."

- to let go of limiting beliefs
- to let go of needing approval
- to let go of needing to fit in with the "in-crowd"
- to let go of the narrative that one is born innately inadequate.

Instead, I learned to shift to a space of wholeness.

When I communicate with the Goddess, I feel on two levels. My awareness opens. And, I feel embraced. Yes, I feel this hug on the physical level.

Would you like to make a daily time to open the door to the Goddess's embrace?

* * * * * *

We have seen how letting go is crucial in moving forward and welcoming the Goddess's Embrace. Now let's talk about developing **resilience** for those things we can't let go of.

HOW WITCHES DEVELOP THEIR EXTREME RESILIENCE

How is your resilience?

"To be resilient is to be able to withstand or recover quickly from difficult conditions." – Oxford Languages

Years ago, I was forced to become resilient. I was diagnosed with ITP (Idiopathic Thrombocytopenic Purpura). Basically, my body was at risk of bleeding out just from a bump against a desk or even a chair. I had to be hospitalized, and the ultimate solution was to remove my spleen. But during that tough 30-day period, they took me off my depression medication.

It was an awful experience.

Going through something like that showed me that I was capable of being more resilient than I thought.

Here are three insights.

Insight #1: Realize It Is Possible To Endure And Thrive

Recently, I was studying a microorganism called a tardigrade, also known as a water bear. This creature is famous for surviving extreme conditions, like subzero temperatures, heat hotter than boiling water, and even the vacuum of space. While I certainly didn't want to experience of 30 days in the hospital, my point is that it's possible to endure and still thrive.

In the years following my hospital stay, I learned the value of *the Tree of Life meditation.*

Insight #2: Understand The Significance Of The Tree Of Life Meditation

In this meditation, you imagine roots extending from your feet down into Mother Earth. At the same time, you stretch your branches up through your crown chakra into the universe. This practice connects you to the earth below and the universe above. It's where real power resides for enduring and thriving.

When you're ready, find a quiet space. Make sure this is a place where you are safe and you will not be disturbed.

(You can record your voice on your phone and play it back so you can concentrate on this meditation.)

When you're ready to begin, place your feet flat on the ground, and breathe deeply.

Feel the tension and stress in your body. In a moment, you'll use the following Tree of Life Meditation to release this tension.

The Tree of Life Meditation

Slowly breathe in and out.

Breathe in the energy of love and peace (envision this as white energy). Breathe out all stress and negativity (imagine this as black smoke).

Keep taking deep breaths in and out.

Concentrate on the white energy being breathed in and filling up your body with loving energy. Then let go and breathe out the negative energy you see, in your mind's eye, as black smoke. As you do this, release the stresses of the day. Repeat this breathing cycle at least three times until you are comfortable and relaxed.

As your body and mind begin to relax, continue deep breathing and focus on this mental image:

Envision roots made up of energy that sprout from the bottoms of your feet. With each breath, extend the roots farther and farther down toward Mother Earth.

Extend them down through the floor and down deep into Mother Earth's body. Reach down to Her core, to the center of Her heart.

Once there, with each breath in, pull up the energy from Mother Earth. Breathe out the stress and breathe in the blue-green energy of Mother Earth.

Pull the energy up through your roots, up past the plumbing of the house, past the floor, and into your feet. The energy feels clean and refreshing.

Breathe in deeply. Pull the blue-green energy up into your legs and past your knees. Pull it up, up into your Root Chakra at the base of your spine. Let it fill your body, up into your Sacral Chakra, and continuing to your Solar Plexus Chakra. Breathing in deeply, draw the energy up into your Heart Chakra. Let the energy flow down your arms and into your hands. Feel your body relax as the energy fills it.

Breathing in, draw the energy up into your Throat Chakra.

Concentrate on the blue-green energy filling your body. When you are ready, with another breath in, breathe the energy up into your Third Eye Chakra.

Using your breath, draw the energy up into your Crown Chakra. Feel the energy flow through your body.

With another breath in, pull the energy up and out of your head. The energy forms like branches toward the Sky above you. Continue and let the branches flow up and out into the cosmos.

Draw down the golden energy of the Sun and universe into you. Continue to let the Sky energy intermingle and mix with the Earth energy that is already there. Pull it down through your body and into your arms.

Continue breathing deeply, mixing and pulling the energies down to your Heart Chakra.

Breathe in again, pulling the energy of the universe down into your Solar Plexus Chakra.

Continue pulling in the energy. Let it flow into you. Pull it into your Root Chakra. Breathing deeply, pull it down your legs and down to your feet.

Feel the energy from both the Earth Mother and the Sun Father that is within you.

Now focus on pulling this mixed energy out from the top of your head once more. But this time let it cascade down all around you like a waterfall until it completely surrounds you.

With a deep breath in, take the energy and push it out in all directions into an egg shape around you. This is the Cosmic Egg of Protection.

Keep breathing and push out more and more energy into your egg.

Your egg gets stronger and stronger.

When you are satisfied with the strength of your egg stop and relax.

In a moment or two, slowly start to pull your branches back within you, pulling them in with each breath.

Let any extra energy dissipate through the roots that you had placed into the Earth from your feet, keeping the egg intact.

Now breathe in, pulling the roots up, and back into your body just like the branches that were above you. Give yourself over to the total relaxation you now feel.

In a moment or two—and when you are ready—open your eyes.

This meditation helps you remember that you are more than just your body. You are connected to the Gods and the universe.

Insight #3: Ask The Gods To Guide You Through Prayer

Here is a prayer you can use for guidance and support:

Hornlord of the Greenwood, Lady of the Silver Moon
Guide me through my troubles.
Lift me up so I can endure and thrive.
So I can flourish and truly be alive.
So Mote It Be.

Let's Pull This All Together

- Realize it is possible to endure and thrive.
- Understand the significance of the Tree of Life meditation.
- Ask the Gods to guide you through prayer.

* * * * * *

Here is another great meditation to help you on your path.

HEAL FROM BEING BROKEN – A MEDITATION

This Guided Meditation is from my 300th Episode on my podcast Goddess Has Your Back available at Spotify, Apple Podcasts, and Podbean. It is also available on my blog at Goddess Has Your Back dot com.

This is a Guided Meditation for Witches.

Please ensure you are in a safe, quiet space where you will not be disturbed. Silence your phone and any notifications.

You can record this meditation on your phone in your voice for later listening.

Let's begin.

Close your eyes.
Take a deep breath in… and out.
Breathe deeply.
Relax.

Let go of the stress of the day.
Breathe in relaxation.
Breathe out tension.

You are still aware of the light in the room.
Now, the light begins to fade, and as it fades,

you feel a sense of total comfort.

You are safe.
You are secure.
You are held in the stillness of the darkness.

Now, a new light forms.
You feel warm and safe in this light.
Soon, you notice a stairway descending before you.

You reach out and gently grab the banister.
You take a deep breath...
and step down.

Step by Step, You Relax...

Step down once — your worries drift away.
Breathe in... and out.
Step down again — your mind becomes quiet.
Breathe in... and out.
Step down again — your shoulders, face, and head relax.
Your arms relax.
Step down again — your chest, stomach, and legs relax.

Breathe deeply.
You feel calm and safe.
Step down again — your mind is at ease.
Step down once more — your body is completely relaxed.

You are now in total relaxation.

You arrive at the bottom of the staircase.
You are surrounded by a soft mist.

When the mist clears, you find yourself in a forest.
It's nighttime, and the night is warm and comfortable.
The sky is clear, and stars sparkle above.
A full moon glows gently in the night sky.

You notice a path ahead of you in the forest.

You move easily down the path.

You feel a cool breeze caress your skin.
You smell frankincense and myrrh in the air.
You hear crickets singing all around.

You arrive at a beautiful clearing.
There before you is a temple—radiant and ancient.
This is the Temple of the Gods.

Two large doors open by themselves.
Inside, you see the God and the Goddess waiting for you.
They smile and beckon you forward.

You move toward Them, feeling Their loving presence.
They lead you into the temple, into a great hall.

In the center of the room is a giant cauldron.
A fire flickers and crackles within.
The flames are hypnotic, glowing softly.

To the right, you see an altar.
On it rests a vase holding three white roses.
You also see three small objects placed on a metal pentacle plate.

The God speaks:
"You see these three objects on the plate?
They represent what feels broken inside you."

The Goddess steps forward. She holds a bowl filled with green powder.

She says:
"These are the Healing Sands.
Take a handful and toss it into the flames."

You do.
The flames shift—glowing emerald green.

She continues:
"These are healing flames.

You may now place what is broken within you into the fire.
Watch as it transforms and becomes whole again."

You pick up the first object.
You turn it over in your hands.
How does it feel?
What does this object represent in your life
that needs to be healed?

You gaze deeply into the emerald flames.

You ask the fire to heal the pain you carry with this object.
You toss it into the fire.

The flames shimmer. A green smoke rises.
You feel the pain melt away.

The weight you once carried is lifted.
You feel a new lightness within.

One of the white roses turns a beautiful shade of red.

You pick up the second object.
You turn it over in your hands.
How does it feel?

What does this object represent in your life
that needs to be healed?

You gaze into the flames again.
You ask the fire to heal this part of you.
You toss the object into the fire.
The emerald flames shimmer again.
Green smoke rises.

And once more, the pain melts away.
You feel space and lightness return.

The second white rose turns a warm, glowing red.

Now, you pick up the third and final object.

How does it feel?

What does this object represent in your life
that needs to be healed?

You look deeply into the healing flames.

You ask the fire to transform this pain.

You toss the object in.
The flames shimmer. Green smoke rises.

You feel the pain dissolve.
The burden is gone. You feel peace.

The third and final white rose turns a radiant red.

The God and Goddess smile at you.
You feel lighter, whole, and at peace.

The light in the temple dims.
The fire flickers softly... and then drifts away.

A soft mist forms again around you.
It grows thicker, wrapping you in quiet comfort.

Even in the mist, you feel the love
of the God and Goddess surrounding you.

The mist becomes darkness.

Then—a new light blooms around you.
It becomes brighter... and brighter...

And now, you find yourself back where your journey began.

You feel calm, relaxed, and most of all... whole.

When You're Ready...
You gently return to your body.
Wiggle your fingers. Wiggle your toes.
Bring awareness back into your space.

And when you're ready,
you may open your eyes.

May this healing stay with you—mind, body, and spirit.

Remember you can return to this meditation as needed, as your travel along your sacred path.

* * * * * *

Now, I introduce you to the process of The InstaCircle. The InstaCircle can support you by shielding you from negative energies.

THE INSTACIRCLE

You can quickly cast the InstaCircle.
Here is the InstaCircle process with the movements:

Using your power hand (your dominant hand), trace the Circle three times.

And say,
I cast my Circle thrice,
round, round and round.

Point your index finger up to the heavens and then point it down to the earth, pulling energy down to the ground.

And say,
Let no bane get in,
From heavens to ground.

As I mentioned earlier, the InstaCircle can support you by shielding you from negative energies.

* * * * * *

We began with shielding. Now, we move onto the Insta-Ritual. For many witches, a process like this helps them get the things they need.

THE INSTA-RITUAL

Gather these objects:
- 1 Small white candle (a Mini-Chime Candle)
- Lighter or match
- Candle holder

Think of what you need.

Hold the candle in your hands with that thought. Be as exact as you can in what desired outcome you want.
Then place it in the candle holder, lighting it and saying.

Little candle of mine manifest (the object you desire) for me in no time.

Let the candle burn all the way out.

* * * * * *

Performing this Insta-Ritual is part of building your practice of the Craft.

Now we move onto a breathing exercise.

BREATH OF LOVE

Here is a brief process that helps you celebrate your true gift from the Gods. Breath comes from the Goddess and God. Breath supports and heals you.

So, take a deep breath in, and breathe in the love of the Gods. Hold…

In your mind, say, "I breathe in Love."

Then exhale.
In your mind, picture tension, stress, and pain exiting your body as if you are exhaling black smoke out of your mouth.

In your mind say, "I breath out all stress, pain, and tension."

Repeat this process 9 times.

A warning: As with any form of exercise or exertion, consult with your doctor. Some people may need to be careful about getting lightheaded or hyperventilating.

* * * * * *

What if you could take a better path to financial abundance?

THE BIG MISTAKE ABOUT GOING FOR WEALTH AND MORE (A WITCH'S PERSPECTIVE)

There's a big mistake when it comes to going for wealth and more.

Are you in trouble with money?
Do you spend a lot of time afraid of the future?
Do you buy lottery tickets, wishing and hoping that you'll get wealthy?

Wealth, money, prosperity, and abundance can be confusing for many of us.

Here are three insights.

Insight #1: Be Grateful And Go For More

From a spiritual perspective, we resonate with our divinity when we are grateful.

Even when you're in a space of fear, it's possible to shift into gratitude. One of my spiritual elders falls asleep by silently

chanting in his mind:
"Thank you, God. Thank you, Goddess."

He's grateful for all his blessings.

In a book, titled *The Hidden Power of the And Universe,* author Tom Marcoux reminds us that this is an "and" universe. This means we can hold multiple truths and desires at once.

So, let's remember:
Be grateful and go for more.

Insight #2: Focus On Being, Not Pretending And Seeking

If you tell yourself or others, "I'm seeking financial wealth," and you stay in that mindset... you're just seeking. You're stuck in the seeking.

Researchers have found that many people pretend to be confident. But true confidence does **not** come from pretending, it comes from being.

For witches, that confidence comes from a deeper place:
The God and Goddess placed divinity within you.

So, we focus on being. Not just performing certain behaviors or checking boxes.

Start with being authentic.
Be someone who wants to contribute at work, in your relationships, and in your community.

That's where true confidence is born.
And that kind of confidence is magnetic to wealth.

According to Merriam-Webster, one definition of *wealth* includes:
"an abundance of valuable material possessions or resources."

Let's talk about resources.

Divinity is within you. That's your source: Your ability to make connections, to build relationships, and to grow in prosperity.

Focus on being:
- Being kind
- Being helpful
- Being respectful
- Being useful both at work and in your community

Focus on being, and you open the door to wealth... and more.

Insight #3: Pray To The Gods

Here's a prayer you can use:

Blessed Lord and Lady,
Help me focus on what truly matters in my life, now and in the future.
Help me be true to myself and my journey.
In this truth, I attract financial abundance and wealth.
I live in full well-being.
So Mote It Be.

Let's Pull This All Together

The big mistake when it comes to going for wealth and more is this:
Starting from the outside.

It's a mistake to start by pretending you're confident... pretending you're making a contribution.

Instead, to attract wealth:
- Start with gratitude
- Focus on being: Being authentic, being kind, being

useful

And it all starts with meditation, ritual, and the deep knowing that:
The God and the Goddess placed divinity within you.

That is true wealth.

The God and Goddess delight in supporting you, as you stay grateful and go for more.

May these insights support your path.

* * * * * *

So go for more, **AND** be sure to start with gratitude.
Now, let's explore the expansive Witch's Vision

HOW WITCHES KEEP THEIR WITCH'S VISION

How is your vision?
Do you have difficulty seeing?

I know an artist whose vision started to go, slowly, subtly. It turned out to be cataracts. Because it happened gradually, she didn't even realize how bad it had gotten... until it was nearly gone.

That's the danger with vision, both physical and spiritual. **When it fades little by little, we often don't notice until we've lost something important.**

As witches, we must protect our Witch's Vision.

Here are three insights for you.

Insight #1: Realize The Difference Between Expansive Vision And Constricted Vision

A witch's vision is expansive.

But many human groups—religious, political, cultural—have narrow perspectives. They define themselves by being **not** like others. That creates tunnel vision, a constricted way of seeing the world: "We're right. They're wrong."

That's NOT the Way of the Goddess.

The Goddess wants you to see and know your true self, the one that exists beyond fear, beyond labels, beyond limits.

To maintain an expansive vision, stay awake and alert. Notice the people and systems that try to trap you in narrow thinking.

Protect your inner sight.
Write rituals and prayers.
Do meditations that help you ease into your essence.
Let your experience of your spirit expand.

Insight #2: Access Your Intuition

Think of your intuition like flowing water: Gentle, adaptable, alive.

Certain forces in our world want us to rely only on our intellect to overthink, overanalyze, and forget to feel. But the Witch's Vision includes intuition as sacred.

Witches understand nature.
Nature moves in seasons and cycles.
Not everything is linear or logical. And that's okay.

Here's something to consider:
Depending on how we observe it, light behaves as a particle or a wave.
That truth doesn't fit neatly into the rational mind. But as witches, we're not limited by logic alone.

We hold space for nature, physics, and magick.

Insight #3: Invite The Goddess To Support Your Expansive Vision

The Goddess wants to support you.
She wants you to remember who you are.

Here's a prayer you can use.

Lady of the Moon,
Expand my sight,
So that I may experience my true self.
So Mote It Be.

The Goddess loves to hear from you.
She and the God created you, and They want the best for your journey.

So, continue to pray.
Continue to write your rituals.
Continue to meditate and connect with your true vision.

Let's Pull This All Together

- Realize the difference between expansive vision and constricted vision.
- Access your intuition—it's a vital part of your witch's sight.
- Invite the Goddess to support your expansive vision.

Your Witch's Vision is sacred. Keep it open. Keep it clear. Keep it yours.

* * * * * *

As witches we do our Craft. Here are some actions to ensure safety.

HOW WITCHES PUT IN SAFEGUARDS AND ATTEMPT A SPELL

Spell Safeguards

One of my spiritual elders told me about an experience. Judy did a spell but forgot to dismiss all the elements. She missed the Element of Water. Soon after, she had terrible trouble with the plumbing in her building. Water was everywhere.

This reminds us that when we do a spell, when we wield our magick, we're doing something powerful.

Even in the mundane world, we need to be careful with power. People are careful about electricity. They're careful about fire. And magick deserves the same level of care.

Here are four insights.

Insight #1: "For This Or Better"

The Gods know what is best for us.
Sometimes we do a spell, and we can't perceive all the consequences. So, as a safeguard, we add the phrase:
"For this or better."

So, you're doing your spell. As part of your chant, after you say what you want, express:

"For this or better."

Insight #2: "For The Good Of All Involved"

Wiccans are aware of the Threefold Law:
Whatever you put out into the universe comes back threefold—three times the power.

That's why it's wise to say:
"For the good of all involved."

This helps ensure your magick flows in harmony with the greater good.

Insight #3: Dismiss Any Entities You Summon

Remember Judy? This is exactly what happened to her. She didn't dismiss the Element of Water.

When you invite entities or Elements into your Circle, be sure to thank them and dismiss them when the work is done.

It's a sign of respect. It also keeps your space clear.

Insight #4: Ask The Goddess For Protection

Include these words in your spell:
"Goddess, protect me and all involved, during and after this spell."

The Goddess loves you. She and the God are waiting for your invitation. So, ask for Their help.

Let's Pull This All Together

Whenever you do a spell, part of the process is putting in

safeguards. These are four powerful ones:

- For this or better
- For the good of all involved
- Dismiss any entities you summon into your Circle
- Ask the Goddess for protection

* * * * * *

Doing magick is a gift from the Gods. But what happens when you have barriers impeding your success? How can you remove such problems?

HOW WITCHES REMOVE THE BARRIERS TO USING MAGICK

Do you ever feel squeezed by stress? Sometimes, it hits me first thing in the morning. It can throw off the whole day. Maybe I get a phone call from a family member, or something unexpected happens that forces me to leave the house early. I miss my morning coffee, and suddenly, I'm already feeling stressed.

Here are three insights.

Insight #1: Develop The Skills To Handle Stress Or Risk Missing The Precious Moment.

Over the years, I've learned that if I don't do something every day to manage my stress, it blocks me from being fully present in the moment. For example, this morning, I woke up with a bad spasm in my back, and it drained my energy all day.

To handle stress, I've built a daily practice of stretching, walking, and having quiet time. If I skip any of these, it's like letting the "mud" of stress in. It affects everything. The key is to develop daily practices that keep us free and present. I often call the present moment the "precious moment."

Insight #2: Stress Can Put Up A Wall Between You And Your Magick.

Magick is all about creating and moving energy. When you're stressed, it can feel like you're all bunched up. That creates a barrier between you and your ability to manifest what you want.

Manifesting with magick already takes focus and energy, but stress makes it twice as hard. That's why daily practices to handle stress and release tension are so important.

Insight #3: Invite The Gods To Deepen Your Practice.

Here's a prayer that can support your journey:

Lord of the Wildwood, Lady of the Moon,
Guide me to the answers I seek.
Help me wash away the stresses of my life.
Guide me in my daily practices to keep my body, mind, and soul light,
warm, and positive. May my practice of magick be elevated.
So Mote It Be

May this prayer support your path.

Let's Pull This All Together

- Develop the skills to handle stress or risk missing the precious moment.
- Stress can create a barrier between you and your magick.
- Invite the Gods to deepen your practice.

* * * * * *

Taking down barriers to your magick is crucial. Here's

something also vital to your personal energy and fulfillment. Be sure to avoid a false soulmate...

HOW WITCHES AVOID THE FALSE SOULMATE

Recently, my friend Amanda was telling me about someone she's dating. She said, "We like Chinese food. We like horror movies. I'm in love."

Have you noticed that's how we often get relationships started? We find people with similar interests, and suddenly it feels like a lifetime commitment. But is it?

Here are three insights.

Insight #1: Identify The Projections Of Lost Parts Of Your Soul

As a child, what did you want to be when you grew up? Are you doing that now? Many of us lose parts of ourselves over the years.

Have you ever been at a party and found yourself really attracted to someone? It's possible that what drew you to them was a part of yourself that you once had or maybe even wanted years ago.

For example, if you consider yourself a quiet person and wish you were more sociable, you might find yourself attracted to someone who appears outgoing. The truth is, when you're comfortable with your friends, you're probably sociable, too. You're just not showing that side with everyone.

The false soulmate is made up of your projections. These projections aren't real. They're parts of you that you're not seeing clearly. You might meet someone new and think they're really great at talking, but what if they're just wearing a public mask?

So, when two people meet, it's projections meeting projections. How do you get to the real you and the real them?

You need time.
You have to spend enough time together to let each person show who they really are. This is what we call the undefended self.

Let's face it. Dating can often feel like auditioning for a role. You only show what you think will get you the part. That's why it's so important to pause and reflect on what you may have lost from your own soul. Healing yourself first is vital, because infatuation often comes with a lot of unreal aspects.

Insight #2: Make Space To Unmask The Real Person

Have you ever noticed how, after a while, you might start testing the other person? You reveal something about yourself, maybe an uncomfortable family situation, and wait to see how they respond. This is part of the unmasking process: Both of you showing who you really are.

As witches, we know that in each lifetime, we've set a plan for ourselves. This life is for learning something specific. Before we incarnate, there are certain souls that agree to play roles in our lives. Some people refer to this as soul groups.

The important thing to understand is that you have a soul destiny. Part of that destiny is to unmask yourself. You'll also take enough time for the other person to do the same.

Insight #3: Express A Prayer To The Goddess

Here's a prayer that you can use.

Lovely Lady of the Moon,
Strengthen me so I heal and become whole.
Strengthen me so I can support my partner in healing and becoming whole.
So Mote It Be.

To express your soul and support someone else's soul is important work. It takes effort, patience, and space to develop wisdom.

The way to avoid the false soulmate is to pay close attention to yourself. Look for the parts of you that have been lost along the way. We often desire someone else to make things easy. That includes someone who expresses the parts we're missing so we don't have to work on them ourselves.

But we need to pay attention to our own soul. Take time each week to discover the parts of yourself that need exploration and expression.

Let's Pull This All Together

- Identify the projections of lost parts of your soul.
- Make space to unmask the real person.
- Express a prayer to the Goddess.

* * * * * *

Soulmates are special and finding the right one is important. But what are mistakes that can cause you tremendous trouble?

HOW WITCHES AVOID MISTAKES THEY CAN'T BOUNCE BACK FROM

When I was 10, I spent a lot of time at a place called Henley's Rock. It was a spot where you could climb different parts of the rock and just have fun.

One day, my friend, Amy, and I walked at Henley's Rock. We were surprised when two young rock climbers offered to show us how to climb a specific part of the rock. At 10, we were light, athletic, and could follow instructions easily.

Five years later, Amy and I returned to the rock to climb again. But this time, things were different. Puberty had changed our bodies. We were heavier in some places, and climbing didn't feel as easy. Amy, being Amy, taunted me to climb the rock first. So, I started climbing, but my inner voice said, "This isn't working."

Amy pushed me aside and decided to climb it herself. She got stuck halfway up. Amy couldn't go up or down. I rushed to get help from some rock climbers on the other side, and they came over to help her down.

I learned a lot from that experience.
I have three insights to share with you.

Insight #1: Observe Your Own Ego

Amy's ego was on fire that day. She wanted to prove something. But I listened to the quiet voice within. Sometimes, we need to really pause and listen to ourselves. If we follow someone else's lead, we might end up getting hurt. And some kinds of hurt, you can't bounce back from.

As witches, we realize that we are connected to the Gods and the universe. We don't need to prove ourselves or get stuck in our egos. Or stuck on a rock.

Insight #2: Listen To Yourself And Say "No"

Amy kept pressing me to climb, but I listened to myself and the quiet voice within. I said, "No, I'm not doing it."

If I had followed her lead, neither of us would have been able to get help. We both could've fallen and seriously injured ourselves. Maybe I wouldn't even be here today.

Do you take time to listen to yourself?

Insight #3: Listen To Your Mentors

When I was 10, the young rock climbers were my mentors. But as I got older, I needed new mentors. My body had changed, and I had to learn how to use it differently. As we mature, we also need to protect ourselves from injury like overstretching, tearing tendons, or damaging tissues.

The true mentors that stay with us are the Gods. As human beings, there's so much we don't see from our perspective. A friend of mine once said that he can't see the back of his head, which is probably a good thing since he's missing hair.

He has a great sense of humor about it.

The point is: To improve in life, we need mentors. You can always call upon the Gods.

Have you noticed that everyone has certain quirks and tendencies? Many of us develop habits based on how we were raised. But as the years go by, we discover we need new behaviors to continue growing. Staying stuck in the way you were when you were 10 doesn't help as you mature.

Meditation truly helps you. Ask the Gods for new perspectives. Ask for Their support to help you let go of what no longer serves you.

Let's Pull This All Together

- Observe your own ego.
- Listen to yourself and say "no."
- Listen to your mentors.

PART 5. SHIFT TO THE GODDESS PATH

What is easy? To walk the path of the ego. A number of authors and spiritual elders suggest that the ego is made of fear. It's the part that wants you to stay small and safe.

What would it be like to shift to the Goddess Path? Imagine expanding your horizon. Seeing more. Perceiving things with true clarity. And, knowing, in your heart, what your soul calls you to do.

Let's explore this...

BREAK THROUGH LOW SELF-ESTEEM TO WHAT YOU REALLY WANT (A WITCH'S PERSPECTIVE)

Are you happy?
And... do you feel worthy of happiness?

I deal with depression symptoms. For me, it's like having an enemy in my own head. One that keeps kicking me and saying, "You're not worthy of happiness."

Recently, I went to a spiritual elder in my circle, and we did a process together. Through a series of questions, we went down 11 levels. What I discovered was a kind of map of how I think.

Like many human beings, I started with something surface-level, just a slight hint of what I really feared.

This experience was a revelation.
I have three insights to share with you.

Insight #1: View What Is Possible

Let's begin with a definition of *self-esteem.*

Nathaniel Branden said:
"Self-esteem is the disposition to experience oneself as being competent to cope with the basic challenges of life—and of being worthy of happiness."

Well, that sounds like a big challenge to me.

Depression symptoms can strangle my feelings of accomplishment... and my feelings of competence. But having gone through the 11 levels with my spiritual elder, I realized something important:
If I don't feel competent, I don't feel worthy of happiness.

Let's pause here for a moment. Imagine what the Goddess would say to me.

Would she tell me I'm not worthy of happiness because I have depression symptoms?
Would she say I'm not worthy because I have doubts?

No.

She would help me see that something is possible.

For example:
- I can have moments of happiness.
- I can have moments of feeling competent.

One example? Uploading a podcast episode that my team and I create gives me a great moment. I feel like I accomplished something.

So even in the middle of depression symptoms, I can experience moments of good self-esteem.

Insight #2: Let The Goddess Show You The Essence

Again, imagine what the Goddess would say to you.
Would She tell you you're worthless?

Absolutely not.

She would say, "I put divinity within you."
And that's something you can experience in the present moment.

The ego tries to make us feel small.
But the Goddess helps you see the essence of the situation.
You are worthy.

She placed divinity within you. That truth is your foundation.

Insight #3: Say A Prayer To The Goddess

Here's a prayer you can use:

Goddess,
Reveal the essence of my path.
Strengthen me.
Guide me to this present moment.
Help me know I am worthy of happiness.
So Mote It Be.

Let's Pull This All Together

Your ego, that part of you made of fear, is **not** your essence.

The Goddess placed divinity within you.
That divinity knows the truth:
  • You do have moments of competence.
  • You are worthy of happiness.

May these insights support your path.

* * * * * *

Low self-esteem can really screw you up. And fear is part of that.
So how do we handle fear?

HOW WITCHES STOP FEAR FROM TRASHING THEIR DAY

Do you ever wake up in the morning, and your thoughts make your heart race? Do you feel bad or afraid?

Sometimes when I wake up, my first thoughts are about things I've done wrong or mistakes I've made. That can put me in a bad mood. It can easily trash my whole day.

Here are three insights.

Insight #1: Identify Automatic Fear Thoughts

The first step to elevating your life is awareness. It helps you identify your automatic fear thoughts.

For example, my friend, Kelsey, wakes up, remembers she has a job interview, and immediately thinks, *"Oh, I'll screw up like I did last time."* So, she pauses and notices how her mind automatically goes to that. The truth is, when you're aware of something, you can do something about it.

Over the years, many books have emphasized confronting your non-useful thoughts. But I've learned that if I directly confront a thought like "I'm stupid," it doesn't really help.

What actually works for me is **moving my focus.**

Insight #2: Move Your Focus

Some mornings I wake up this way. My first thoughts are that I have a meeting and everything's going to go wrong or that I'm going to look like an idiot. Or both.

This is when I need to move my focus.

Challenging my thoughts doesn't work for me. If I say, *"I'm stupid,"* and then I challenge it by saying, *"No, I'm not,"* and citing evidence like, "I've written nine books," my depression symptoms tend to block that evidence.

I was talking about this with a friend recently. I said, *"I've written nine books,"* but the depression symptoms block me from feeling good about that accomplishment. What helps me is **moving my focus. I focus on the Goddess**.

I'm not trying to make myself feel better by citing evidence. I'm actually redirecting my attention to the truth of the Goddess.

Insight #3: Connect With The Gods

When I need to move my focus, I say something like, *"Lord and Lady, help me to..."* That's how I begin my communication with Them.

A friend of mine says that when he needs to sleep, he repeats three words in his mind: *"God, thank you."* He says that puts him in a space of higher power and gratitude.

So, I invite you to pick your favorite phrases. Once again, I say, *"Lord and Lady, help me to..."* and then I finish my prayer.

Let's Pull This All Together

- Identify automatic fear thoughts.
- Move your focus.
- Connect with the Gods.

* * * * * *

We have explored the process of moving our focus. We *can* focus on the Goddess. An important process is to discover what spiritually nourishes you.

HOW WITCHES DISCOVER WHAT IS SPIRITUALLY NOURISHING TO THEM

A Reflection on Authentic Spiritual Growth

Have you ever noticed your habits at a restaurant?

For me, it's raw tomatoes. I always take them out. Every single time. I just don't like them. That small action got me thinking about nourishment, not just of the body, but of the soul.

Just as we choose what we feed our bodies, we also choose what we feed our spirit.

Here are three insights on how to truly nourish your spiritual self.

Insight #1: Find The Gaps In Your Spiritual Nutrition

A well-rounded spiritual life is like a balanced meal. It includes different practices: Prayer, ritual, and meditation. And, you pay attention to messages you discover in the present moment.

Including what you find in this book.

Ask yourself:
- What am I currently feeding my spirit?
- What's missing?

Sometimes we lean heavily into just one area, like meditation, because it feels good. But spiritual growth isn't just about feeling good. It's also about recognizing what's lacking and intentionally filling in those nutritional gaps.

Insight #2: Eat Your Greens

Think of this as a metaphor. Just like spinach, kale, or in my case, cauliflower and those dreaded raw tomatoes, some spiritual practices are uncomfortable. But they're essential.

Real growth means doing the hard things:
- Getting unstuck.
- Facing old wounds.
- Starting a new chapter of life.

Spiritual comfort alone isn't enough. If all we do is stay in our comfort zone, it's like skipping the veggies of life. We're missing the fuel that pushes us toward transformation.

This is where spiritual elders, wise friends, and mentors come in. They challenge us to face reality, to move through the pain, and not around it.

Insight #3: Be Aware Of Bliss-Out Versus Facing Reality

Yes, bliss is beautiful. Retreats, rituals, elevated states—they're real and meaningful. But true spiritual growth requires that we don't hide in the bliss.

Ever meet someone who just came back from a retreat, and they're glowing? But totally disconnected? They avoid talking about anything "messy" because it might kill their buzz.

That's not balance.

There's a powerful quote by Alistair Cooke:
"A professional is someone who can do his best work when he doesn't feel like it."

This applies to your spiritual path, too. It's not about waiting to feel inspired or peaceful. It's about showing up anyway.

Consider the story of the therapist who urged a woman to be patient with her partner. But her partner was a rageaholic, unwilling to change. Patience wasn't the answer. Leaving was.

Sometimes, the most spiritual thing you can do is make a hard decision. That's what we mean by facing reality.

Let's Pull This All Together

To experience real spiritual nourishment, you need:

- **Self-awareness** – Find the gaps in your practice. Are you leaning too much into comfort? Are you neglecting a core element like ritual, study, or mentorship?

- **Discipline** – Learn to eat your greens. Lean into practices that stretch you. Step into the discomfort that leads to transformation.

- **Discernment** – Know the difference between bliss-out and necessary suffering on the path of growth. Are you using spirituality to avoid pain—or to move through it?

Think of a tree. It can't grow without soil, sun, and rain.

Likewise, you can't grow spiritually without the full range of nourishment—light, shadow, peace, and challenge.

Ask yourself:
- Where am I spiritually undernourished?
- What "greens" have I been avoiding?
- Am I seeking bliss at the expense of truth?

Let your answers guide your next steps.

Here's a Quick Recap

- Find the gaps in your spiritual nutrition

- Eat Your Greens; embrace uncomfortable practices

- Be aware of bliss-out versus facing reality

May you find the nourishment your soul truly needs.
And may you have the courage to take in every part of the meal—even the bitter greens.

* * * * * *

Spiritual nutrition is the key to a better spiritual path. Sometimes saying "NO" is a good thing to keep us on the right track.

HOW YOU CAN SAY "NO" FROM A STRONG BASE (A WITCH'S PERSPECTIVE)

I don't say "no" enough.
A lot of times, I feel kind of spineless.
But there have been times when I said "no" with strength. And I've thought a lot about what made those moments different.

So now, I'm sharing three insights about how to say "no" from a place of spiritual and personal power.

Insight #1: Strengthen Your Inner "Yes" So You Have The Power To Say "No"

I have a friend, Sophie, whose mother is incredibly rude on the phone.
At certain times, Sophie has shown real strength by saying "no" to her mom.

She'll say,
"Okay, that's enough. I'm going to leave this call now. Good night."

Click.

Sophie has learned how to strengthen her **inner yes.**

She's saying "yes" to the divinity and value that the Gods have placed within her.
She's honoring her time, her energy, her boundaries.
And she won't let anyone, even family, drain her energy.

Sophie's strength to say "no" comes from a strong **inner yes** to honoring her inner divinity.

Insight #2: Celebrate Your Strengths Like Facets Of A Diamond

When I think of the God and Goddess, I see them as facets of divinity.
And we, too, have many beautiful facets—just like a diamond.

We are mothers, fathers, siblings, friends, leaders, helpers, creatives, healers.
We are kind. We are strong.
We are people who bring light and positive contribution to the world.

In our rituals and our prayers, we celebrate our strengths—these facets.
When we do that, we build a strong base from which we can say "no" with confidence.

- We say no to abuse.
- We say no to energy drains.
- We say no to being disrespected or degraded.

And **we say yes to positive growth, self-respect, and personal power.**

Insight #3: Pray To The Gods

Here's a prayer you can use to strengthen your "yes," so your "no" becomes powerful:

Goddess,
Help me strengthen my yes,
So that my no is powerful.
Thank you for all the value and divinity
You have placed within me.
God,
Give me Your strength and power to love myself.
Let me have joy for all my facets.
So Mote It Be.

Let's Pull This All Together

We're often told to say no to toxic people or negative energy. But where does the strength to say "no" really come from?

It comes from your **inner yes**.
- Say yes to your worth.
- Say yes to your divinity.
- Say yes to loving yourself.

And from that place of deep self-respect and connection with the Gods, your "no" becomes not just possible, it becomes sacred.

* * * * * *

Say yes to yourself, and the Gods can change your world. The Goddess can reveal many gifts to you.

SEE WHAT THE GODDESS REVEALS (A WITCH'S PERSPECTIVE)

"I feel so vulnerable," Sheri, a friend, said.
I nodded. I deeply related to this.
I reflected on this later.

What if we could align ourselves with Goddess? What if we could know Her power?
And, we can!

The Goddess and God placed divinity within us.
That is our essential identity. Yes, our essence.

Here is something that stands out: **the Goddess's Principles**.
Here is a definition of a *principle*:

A principle is a fundamental truth or proposition that serves as the foundation for a system of belief or behavior or for a chain of reasoning. – Oxford Languages

We can find some of Goddess's principles as she speaks in the writing of Doreen Valiente:

"Keep pure your highest ideal; strive ever towards it; let naught stop you or turn you aside. … Let My worship be within the heart that rejoices, for behold, all acts of love and pleasure are My rituals. And

therefore let there be beauty and strength, power and compassion, honor and humility, mirth and reverence within you." – The Goddess speaking in The Charge of the Goddess, *written by Doreen Valiente*

Here is a prayer to support you in your own identity.

My Gracious Goddess,
Show me my own beauty and strength,
My own power and compassion,
Let me strive for honor and humility, mirth and reverence in all I do.
Let me see myself in You, and You in myself.
So Mote It Be.

* * * * * *

As we embrace the Goddess's Principles, it is time for us to seek Her viewpoint.

EMBRACE COMPASSION WITH THE GODDESS'S VIEWPOINT

Have you noticed so many people who are upside down? They don't have any idea about compassion and strength that the Goddess describes.

I remember The Goddess's words:

"I give peace and freedom…My love is poured upon the earth…Let there be beauty and strength, power and compassion, honour and humility, mirth and reverence within you." – The Goddess in The Charge of the Goddess, *written by Doreen Valiente).*

When I think of people who operate in a way that is opposite of the Goddess's words… I realize we're talking about toxic people. They drain our precious energy.

Ever feel you don't have the energy to do a proper ritual or even just get your projects done?

We, witches, know that words have magick to them.
Carefully consider your own words.

How about these positive words…?
- I am taking good care of myself.
- In meditation, I ask for Goddess's guidance so I take

good care of myself.
- I set boundaries and limit my exposure to toxic people.
- I know that protecting my energy is following the Goddess Path. She wants me to express the best of the divinity she placed within me.

Let's all take good care of ourselves and each other.

* * * * * *

Have you imagined what might be the highest advice from the Goddess?
Let's explore this...

HOW WITCHES FOLLOW THE HIGHEST ADVICE FROM THE GODDESS

"My highest ideal would be to get more sleep," my friend, Kiley, said.

We laughed about this. Still, I know she was using humor connected to a powerful quote...

"Keep pure your highest ideal; strive ever toward it; let naught stop you or turn you aside." – *the Goddess in* The Charge of the Goddess *as written by Doreen Valiente*

Here are three insights.

Insight #1: Become Aware Of "Your Highest Ideal"

Do you know what your highest ideal is? What do you strive for? Is it to serve your community? Or is it simply about "Can I just be awake and on time for work on Mondays?"

Sometimes, it's not obvious. We can struggle to find our meaning related to excellence. Your highest ideal is connected to excellence.

In another spiritual path, it is said that what is inside you can save you or destroy you. What I get from this is: If we don't use our gifts, we might fall apart inside. That's the idea of "destroy you." You need to nurture your gifts and yourself.

What are your gifts?

Take steps each week to support "your highest ideal."

What does it mean to "keep pure your highest ideal?" Imagine all the resistance you face when you simply want to be yourself and fulfill your life's purpose as a witch. People just don't understand our spiritual path.

As witches, we have a "highest ideal" for each one of us. It's unique for each person. It is the one thing we are supposed to learn. We are meant to grow.

You have a gift to share. By being your true self, you also help others on their paths. So how do you do this? With the Gods' help.

Taking steps each week to support your highest ideal is about…
- Identify your highest ideal.
- Strengthen yourself with ritual, nutrition, sleep, and exercise.
- Do actions that support your highest ideal.

For example, I write each week and create a podcast episode. These are steps that help me express my highest ideal of service to my readers and listeners.

Insight #2: Include The Gods In Your Journey For Your Highest Ideal

Living on the level of your highest ideal can be quite a task. This is the reason I like to ask the God and Goddess for support. You can meditate and ask the Gods for Their help. You can say a prayer like this:

O Lovely Lady and Lord of the Fields,
May you guide me through my intuition.
Speak the sacred silent words of your wisdom into my mind.
Let me flow easily on my path like a rushing river to the sea.
Give me your strength O Lord to accomplish my highest ideal without hindrance.
Give me your wisdom O Lady to accomplish my highest ideal with grace.
May my path be free from useless difficulties.
So Mote It Be.

May these insights support your path.

CONCLUSION: 3 STEPS ON YOUR PATH WITH THE GOD AND THE GODDESS

This book has been designed to be your companion during this difficult time of chaos and fear.

You can continue to use this book beyond this first reading.

The 3 Steps on Your Path with the God and the Goddess include three elements:
Shift – Support – Soul

Step One: Practice Your Ways To Shift

Some ways you can shift include:
- Stop and take 3 to 9 deep belly breaths
- Put your hands on the bare Earth and ground
- Say a prayer to the God and Goddess
- Eat something to change your focus (and this helps you ground as well)

The idea is to shift from rumination.
You can decide to change the direction of your thoughts.
Another way to do that is to pick a phrase that shifts your thoughts.

Perhaps, you might say, "God and Goddess, I am grateful for all the blessings."

Step Two: Call For The Goddess's Support

We all need support.
Invite the Goddess to step in.
She wants the best for you.
You can pray, chant to Her, or meditate.

You can simply talk to Her for guidance.
Even during a stressful day, you can pause. In your mind, say something like:
"Hello Goddess. Please help me breathe in calm.
What is a good decision for me to make now?"

Wait for an appropriate amount of time.
You may be surprised at what benevolent and empowering intuitive thought arises.

Step Three: Nurture Your Soul

It helps to pick something simple.
Perhaps, a ritual bath.
Maybe you listen to some of your favorite music.

My favorite action is walking in nature. As I move, I communicate with the God and Goddess. Because They are present in the forest, river or other wild place.

When you feel overwhelmed, remember you can return to this book for support and guidance.

You can open the book to a random page and seek guidance. You can even ask the Gods to guide you.

Perhaps, you'll ask something like this:

"Goddess, show me what I need to see to bless my life."

Then open a page of this book—at random.

Thank you for interacting with this book.

Blessed Be.

Moonwater

P.S. If you'd like to have more support, I have a related course "World On Fire: How Witches and Wiccans Transcend the Chaos and Find Their Peace." Just go to Goddess Has Your Back dot com forward slash Courses

My blog is at Goddess Has Your Back dot com

My podcast Goddess Has Your Back is available through that website, too.

Also, my podcast is available at Spotify, Apple Podcasts, and Podbean.

More than that, I have 9 additional books available as ebooks, audiobooks, and paperback books.

My books are available through a major online retailer.

Additionally, I have 3 courses available for you at Udemy dot com

Those courses include

* Spiritual Solution for Depression Relief

* Goddess Style Weight Loss

* Beyond the Law of Attraction to Real Magick

I realize that you sought this book because you likely need support.

Let's continue with my other books.

My two most popular books are:

- Goddess Has Your Back
- Beyond the Law of Attraction to Real Magic

Two pragmatic books are:

- Goddess Style Weight Loss
- Goddess Has Answers to Life's Tough Problems

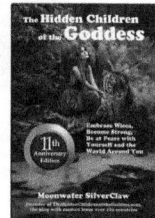

The other 5 books are titled:

- Goddess Walks Beside You
- The Hidden Children of the Goddess - the 2nd Edition
- Be a Wiccan Badass
- Break Free with Goddess
- Goddess Reveals Your Enchanted Light

Thank you for interacting with this book.

Blessed Be.

Moonwater SilverClaw

ACKNOWLEDGEMENT

Thank you to the Goddess and God. I am grateful to my friends and family. Thank you to my team as we serve through my blog, podcast, and books.

Thank you to T.M. for all your support.

ABOUT THE AUTHOR

Moonwater Silverclaw

Moonwater SilverClaw is a Wiccan High Priestess. Her blog at Goddess Has Your Back dot com has readers from over 220 Countries. She is also a member of the Covenant of the Goddess (C.O.G.) and the New Wiccan Church. Moonwater's Podcast Goddess Has Your Back is listed as the #3 podcast of the 15 Best Wicca Podcasts.

Her personal story reveals how Wicca saved her life and helped her strengthen herself to secure her release from an abusive marriage.

At Quora.com, Moonwater is listed as "Most Viewed Writer" in the category "Witchcraft (Historical)" — with over 1.7 million views.

A global speaker, Moonwater is the author of 10 books — although she is dyslexic. She has editors. Moonwater has addressed college students in Comparative Religion for over 10 years.

Moonwater's work is endorsed by notables, including Patrick McCollum (Mahatma Gandhi Award for the Advancement of Religious Pluralism).

Moonwater SilverClaw can be contacted at: AskAWitchNow@gmail.com

Or on her blog: Goddess Has Your Back dot com

www.ingramcontent.com/pod-product-compliance
Lightning Source LLC
Chambersburg PA
CBHW060349090426
42734CB00011B/2079